How to
Make a Soul

How to Make a Soul

The Wisdom of John Keats

✦

Eric G. Wilson

NORTHWESTERN UNIVERSITY PRESS

EVANSTON, ILLINOIS

Northwestern University Press
www.nupress.northwestern.edu

Copyright © 2016 by Eric G. Wilson.
Published 2016 by Northwestern University Press. All rights reserved.

Printed in the United States of America

10   9   8   7   6   5   4   3   2   1

Library of Congress Cataloging-in-Publication Data

Wilson, Eric, 1967– author.
    How to make a soul : the wisdom of John Keats / Eric G. Wilson.
       pages cm.
    Includes bibliographical references and index.
    ISBN 978-0-8101-3194-1 (cloth : alk. paper)—ISBN 978-0-8101-3193-4
(pbk. : alk. paper)—ISBN 978-0-8101-3195-8 (ebook)
    1. Keats, John, 1795–1821. 2. Keats, John, 1795–1821—Criticism and
interpretation. 3. Soul in literature. 4. Melancholy in literature. I. Title.
PR4837.W55 2015
821.7—c23
                                                                2015031423

To my students at the Worrell House,

spring 2012

CONTENTS

A Note to the Reader   *ix*

Chapter 1
Continual Allegory   *3*

Chapter 2
The Delighted Stare   *9*

Chapter 3
Sick Eagle   *15*

Chapter 4
Ethereal Chemical   *23*

Chapter 5
Negative Capability   *29*

Chapter 6
Disinterestedness   *39*

Chapter 7
Mist   *47*

Chapter 8
Sore Throat   *57*

Chapter 9
Leap of the Eye   *67*

Chapter 10
Women   *73*

Chapter 11
Working Salvation   *77*

Chapter 12
Hyperion   *83*

Chapter 13
Fanny   *95*

Chapter 14
Suicide   *99*

Chapter 15
Dream and the Dragon World   *103*

Chapter 16
Soul-Making   *109*

Chapter 17
Psyche   *117*

Chapter 18
Indolence   *121*

Chapter 19
Urn   *125*

Chapter 20
Melancholy   *131*

Chapter 21
Nightingale   *135*

Chapter 22
Autumn   *141*

Chapter 23
A Tear Is an Intellectual Thing   *147*

Chapter 24
I Shall Die Easy   *151*

Notes   *155*

Index   *159*

A NOTE TO THE READER

I spent the spring of 2012 near Keats's Hampstead home. When I visited, I tried to put myself in the place of the ailing poet, especially on the mornings he lay fevered in the main parlor, staring out at the mulberry tree—still alive today—and listening to the birds like a man with only months to live. I also visited the Old Operating Theatre Museum, located on the original site of St. Thomas's Hospital, where Keats studied medicine. In the amphitheater, I squeamishly pictured the amputations he had witnessed. I touched the leather-wrapped surgeon's stick, size of a cane. The patients—there was no anesthesia—bit it to stifle their screams. Their teeth-pocks survive. In April, I drove up to the Lake District, the soggy hills over which Keats and his friend Charles Brown had trudged, much to the detriment of Keats's fragile health, during the summer of 1818. Later, in May, I flew to Rome. I stood in Keats's death room, adjacent to the Spanish Steps. I went to his grave in the Protestant Cemetery. I read "Bright Star" to my ten-year-old daughter and tried not to cry.

I wanted to write a memoir about how these experiences transformed me. But the more I read Keats, the more I realized his most powerful lesson: outstrip the "I." To inhabit imaginatively the being of another, in all of its complexity and nuance: for Keats this is the most animated poetic and ethical state, the ecstasy, Whitmanian, of transcending one's skin, becoming cosmos, from dung beetle to the "journeywork of stars."[1] I discovered that I would best understand my connection to Keats, and to the world, if I negated, as best I could, my ego: let Keats be, and so, *be* Keats, and thus, and here the paradox, be *more* myself, no mere isolated monad, but a man whose contact with creatures close and far, *electrifies*.

This is the power of allegory, a genre that informs my selection of Keats's biographical details. Allegory is a narrative that at its best is a mirror as well as a window, reflection and refraction, whose outward vistas—look at that mountain and all of its struggling climbers—foster new contemplations within: fresh visions of old journeys, and novel quests entirely.

Sometimes you've got to know when to get your ass out of the way and let the world shine by its own light. A friend of mine, a poet, said that, while praising Roethke's "The Heron." He meant that you can see yourself better, your desires and fears, in the flying thing's brightness.

Though I have set aside my purely memoir self, the "I" dominant, this book is still extremely personal, an attempt to reveal the wisdom that spoke so powerfully to me. Personal meditations arise when Keats's own eyes—through which I have tried to see—light on subjects that have seized my being. In his orbs, my experiences in London, the Lake District, and Rome grew, and grow, more luminous; the same is true of my depressions, failures, indolent periods, anxieties, affections, and (so rare) moods of generosity.

I trust that the Keatsian wisdom that so enlivened me will vitalize you, that in the glass of this allegory you will see your most loved and hated parts newly, and reform what you will, and become refreshed. In imagining my life through Keats's, I am also envisioning yours through mine.

An account of Keats's growth of the soul, this book most qualifies as a biography, but, as I have suggested, of a special sort—less historical and more philosophical, focused on those facets that build toward Keats's vision, manifold and vexed, of how to live: vigorously, capaciously, creatively, graciously, with honesty, with gentleness. This doesn't mean hagiography. I reveal the full man, as petty, petulant, stupid, silly, mean, irritable, and sorrowful as the rest of us, but also, with startling and solacing consistency, elastic, funny, charitable, vivacious, brilliant.[2]

The other two primary elements of this book, literary criticism and personal reflection, enter into a relationship of mutual illumination with the life: the verse and the confessions clarify the biography, while the soul-quest brightens what Keats wrote and who I am and want to be.

As a guide to the perplexed, this book aspires to a large audience of intelligent, inquisitive readers who want a more intense existence. But the book will benefit specialists as well. It offers fresh perspectives on Keats's philosophical pragmatism, his uses of irony and comedy, his ethics, his aesthetics.[3]

At the very least, I hope these pages give you what Keats did me: the weird vibrancy of getting over yourself and finding your place in the mystery of another.

How to
Make a Soul

Chapter 1

✦

Continual Allegory

Instead of killing himself, Keats ate a nectarine. This was September 22, 1819. Melancholy generally—though he balanced his blues with a sanguine generosity his many friends admired—Keats was now despondent: "lax, unemployed, unmeridian'd, and objectless,"[1] verging on the anguish that drove him, a year later, to try to poison himself to death. Fortune had flogged him. His guardian's mishandling of his inheritance, combined with his own loose economizing, had left him dangerously in debt, and his best prospect for a job, not promising, was hack journalism. He feared that his chronic sore throat omened the consumption that had killed his mother and brother. (Four months later, his lungs would violently hemorrhage.) And though he had just completed the most productive summer in literary history, which he had capped, twenty-four hours earlier, with the majestic "To Autumn," bad reviews and poor sales of earlier verse portended oblivion. Finally, he was torn up over Fanny Brawne. He "ache[d]" to be with her, would die for only "one hour" at her side, but lacked the nerve to see her when he had the chance. He couldn't "bear flashes of light" and then "return to [his] glooms again."

Keats rallied on this September day to write a letter to his friend Charles Dilke. The poet opens briskly, asking Dilke to arrange new London lodgings for him. But the tone turns sullen. His "temper and imagination" are capriciously flinging him down or up, exhausting his will to do much of anything. He needs to act. If he can't compose poetry, he can at least look to his "immediate welfare." His only vocational hope, though, is journalism, prostitution of intellect.

He continues in this cheerless tone, shuffling peevishly from one complaint to another, bereft of his two most shining virtues, from which sprang his poems and sweet nature: empathy, the ability to feel the world through the body of another, and flexibility, openness to ambiguity, the darkness always bleeding into the light. He is self-absorbed, confused, bitter.

But right smack in the middle of this forlorn letter, after announcing, with strained bonhomie, that he will "fag" (take on menial tasks) until he can afford to "buy Pleasure," Keats chomps fruit: "Talking of Pleasure, the moment I was writing with one hand, and with the other holding to my Mouth a Nectarine—good god how fine—It went down soft pulpy, slushy, oozy—all its delicious embonpoint melted down my throat like a large beatified Strawberry."

The poet dares to eat a peach. He casts Prufrockian despair aside, and, with self-forgetting abandon, blissfully gluts the tongue on the honeyed orange-amber, becoming engulfed while engulfing, relishing the consummation of juice and spit. The communion makes for an *experience*, an instant gone crazily alive: ecstasy only, the going-out of ego into another, the reception of that otherness into the porous sameness of self. Such rapturous tasting is brief salvation, if being saved means overcoming isolation and merging joyously once more the world's flourishing.

Bliss is sensual shock. Keats knew. "I look not for [happiness] if it be not in the present hour—nothing startles me beyond the Moment. The setting sun will always set me to rights, or if a Sparrow come before my Window I take part in its existence and pick about the Gravel."

In another creature, in this case a winged thing, is Keats's virtue restored, his talent for dissolving "I" into "thou." Once Keats was so immersed in Spenser's description of a whale that he, in telling of the passage, "*hoisted* himself up, and looked burly and dominant as he said, '*What an image that is—sea-shouldering whales!*'[2] Another time, the man turned billiard ball, delighting in its "roundness, smoothness[,] volubility & the rapidity of its motion."[3]

The expansion is ecstatically concentric, a ravishing nexus of poet and nectarine quivering inward, to pit and atom, or out: leaf, tree, sun. Keats described this giddy amplification: "I feel more and more every day, as my imagination strengthens, that I do not live in this world alone but in a thousand worlds."

That Keats in munching nectarines and figuring whales could inhabit both his post and the position of the other, and transform this blending into poems unbelievably vital: this is sublime, as was Shakespeare, law-abiding playwright, when he metamorphosed into murderous Macbeth. But even more extraordinary is that Keats could achieve such transcendence while mired in misery.

With one hand Keats loads a note with despair; with the other, he raises fruit, gleefully gulps, floats above woe. How to conceive this capaciousness, this double vision? Does the duplicity disclose a painful rip down the center of the psyche, or signal a mutual arising of interdependent opposites, each side requiring, informing, and intensifying the other? Or is the two-sidedness, impossibly, *both*: terrible tear and gratifying harmony?

A sperm whale, the Ishmael of Melville's novel notes, has eyes on either side of its head, where humans have ears, and so can examine at once "two distinct prospects, one on one side of him, and the other in exactly an opposite direction," as if "a man were able simultaneously to go through the demonstrations of two distinct problems in Euclid." This binary sight intimates a brain "much more comprehensive, combining, and subtle than man's," but precludes a forward unified horizon and so is blind to a straight-on foe, or friend.[4] The line between "first-rate intelligence," Fitzgerald's phrase for a mind holding "two opposed ideas . . . at the same time," and a "crack-up," the novelist's word for going mad, is so fine that it fades.[5]

Leviathan-empathetic and muse of F. Scott, rent between affliction and nectarine, knowing that the sweetened tongue is but a brief respite from the gall that still haunts the taste (as boiled blubber hovers in the nose long after the oil is clear), Keats was keenly, almost preternaturally, sensitive to life's borderlands and their vague lucidities. In his principal moments, miraculous, he harmonized the schizoid and the seamless into lively, lovely, supple, compelling poems. He had a genius for bravely facing and elegantly reconciling to the everyday abrasions and caresses that make up a common life: alarm clocks, deadlines, grudges, Schadenfreude, confusion over stupid shit as well as matters profound, worry over children, pride in trinkets, kindness in spite of ourselves, passion requited and unrequited, occasional bursts before the easel or the blank page—those kinds of things. Exemplifying how to negotiate gracefully among these boring, baffling, exhausting, devastating, exhilarating realities—how to manage them without sinking into despair or sliding into superficiality— Keats blended truth and beauty.

"A man's life of any worth is a continual allegory." So Keats asserted, implying that a noble person's life should be treated like that of a fictional character, an Ishmael or a Hamlet or a Clarissa Dalloway, whose actions aren't accidental and singular but designed, universal. Keats aspired to be such a figure, and I am going to treat him so, not to apotheosize him, but to present him as a model for how to live, how to make a soul.

✦

Embracing the messy surfaces of the material world is typically not associated with that most ancient word, "soul." For Plato, proper care of the soul elevates a person above his prejudices, which seep from the body's anxieties and urges, to a revelation of absolute truth. This soul is attuned to eternity because it descended into matter from there, and to eternity it will return when the anatomy expires.

Compatible with Platonists, Christians believe that God grants each human a soul at birth and communicates with the believer through that soul. The more the devotee practices Christian virtue, the more conversant with God he is, and the more likely his soul to ascend, upon evacuating the corpse, to heaven.

For Platonist and Christian, earthly life is a battle between body and soul, with the body representing ignorance, vice, ugliness, and the soul signaling knowledge, goodness, and beauty. Allegorists from late antiquity through the Renaissance repeatedly represented this conflict. The first such narration, completed by Prudentius around 400 A.D., is called *Psychomachia*, or *The Battle for Man's Soul*. Laying the foundation for later works like *Everyman, The Pearl, Romance of the Rose, Piers Plowman, Pilgrim's Progress*, and *The Faerie Queene, Psychomachia* features seven Christian virtues defeating seven opposing vices.

Viewing Keats's life as allegory, as he would have us do, requires comprehending it as a *psychomachia*. But Keats's fight for his soul differs markedly from the Christian's or the Platonist's. For him the soul isn't an eternal substance, but an aptitude—we cultivate it over a lifetime—for affirming the pains of time and transforming them into meaningful, potent aesthetic forms, which need not be poems or paintings but any practice, from gardening to good parenting, that elegantly ameliorates.

The allegorical Keats blends particular and universal, actual biographical events and a soul-vision elucidating us all. Accidents cohere into narrative concord, an aesthetic whole, with beginning, middle, end; rising and falling action; conflict and resolution; recurring motifs; redemptive apocalypse.

✦

Keats is not a traditional philosopher, but in imagining how we can turn time's breakdowns into conciliating art, he resembles materialist, process-oriented thinkers such as Nietzsche and William James. Like Nietzsche, Keats believes that we can't help but experience the world aesthetically—as opposed to scientifically or spiritually. On an earth thoroughly physical, ultimately unknowable, indifferent to human desires, and disturbingly turbulent, we without thinking translate raw sensual encounters into durable, familiar, significant forms: enabling artifices.

As Wallace Stevens, studied in Nietzsche, put it, we counter reality's pressure with the force of imagination.[6] Life gives us meaningless destruction, the inexorable tick-tick-tick toward death. (A brilliant, contemplative, noble prince named Hamlet senselessly dies). We push back, transforming with our mind the blind, violent ticking into the more solacing tick-tock, tick-tock. (The fallen Dane becomes the friend's poetic occasion: "Now cracks a noble heart—Good night, sweet prince; / And flights of angels sing thee to thy rest.") Not all of us are capable of such wondrous transformations. The greatest thinkers, as Keats and Nietzsche (and Stevens) know, are. They turn life into art; create art that is alive.

James, a professor at Harvard when Stevens was a student there, shares Nietzsche's, and Keats's, emphasis on the value of aesthetic construction. In James's pragmatic vision, no idea is true once and for all. Truth "happens" to those ideas that empower us to live meaningful, graceful lives.[7] To interpret effectively a radically transient, pluralistic world, these ideas must themselves be flexible, varied, subtle, like especially vital artworks. Living pragmatically, we accept the absence of stable truth, embrace the "fictionality" of all so-called facts, and get into the spirit of meaning-making, perpetually evaluating the efficacy of our ideas, revising them when they lose power, creating new ones when the time is right.

Keats resembles Nietzsche and James in kind, but differs from both in degree. Because he is foremost a poet, he is more attuned to the bracing, ambiguous vicissitudes of everyday life—nightingales, gnats, black-eyes, jealousy—than are the philosophers. He takes a more common "ad hoc" attitude toward existence, less interested in how life conforms to theory, and more keen on how this particular moment, unpredictable and irreducibly unique, quickens. His fascination with the concreteness of the quotidian makes him a companionable and efficacious guide to the good life, a familiar physician of the soul.

Chapter 2

✦

The Delighted Stare

On October 9, 1816, Keats, weeks shy of his twentieth birthday and still planning a medical career, invited Charles Cowden Clarke, his closest friend at the time (outside his two brothers), to visit him at his new lodgings on 8 Dean Street. These rooms were conveniently located near Guy's Hospital, where Keats had just completed his surgical training and would soon, if he stuck to his design, become an employee. In the written invitation—his first surviving letter—Keats confesses that his neighborhood, south of the Thames and known as the Borough, is a "beastly place in dirt, turnings, and windings." But there is a clear path through the labyrinth: if Clarke can "run the Gauntlet of London Bridge, take the first turning to the left and then the first to the right," he will find himself at Keats's door, on which he might knock if he is keen on doing "a Charity."

Keats had already passed through labyrinths. When he was eight, his father Thomas, a hostler at London's Swan and Hoop Inn, was thrown from a horse and killed. This was 1804. The mother, Frances, remarried (Gertrude-wise) within three months, and sent John and his three siblings, George, Tom, and Fanny, to live with her parents in Enfield, John and Alice Jennings. From then until the months before her death in 1810, she saw little of the children, essentially orphaning them. When she did return home after falling ill, young John showed remarkable devotion: "He sat up whole nights in a great chair, would suffer nobody to give her medicine but himself, and even cooked her food; he did all, & read novels in her intervals of ease."[1] But his attentions only eased the symptoms of what turned out to be tuberculosis. When he heard of her death while away at his school, the Enfield Academy, the fourteen-year-old fell into "impassioned and prolonged grief; which overcame him so violently that even in the school-room he had to hide himself in an alcove under the master's high desk."[2] The traumas of his mother's absence and early death tortured Keats for the rest of his life. He once told a friend that "his great misfortune had been that from his infancy he had no mother."

Other losses pummeled the Keats children. Grandfather John had died in 1805, and grandmother Alice only lived four years beyond her daughter, succumbing in 1814. Now the children were forced under the guardianship of Richard Abbey, earlier appointed by Alice, who believed him to be responsible and charitable. (He turned out to be anything but, mismanaging the Keats' inheritance, proving stingy with what money was available, and prone to sententious lectures.) John wasn't exaggerating when he later confessed, "I have never known any unalloy'd Happiness for many days together: the death or sickness of someone has always spoilt my hours."

In 1810 Abbey pulled Keats from the academy and placed him under an apothecary's tutelage. Although the years of his medical apprenticeship were "the most placid period in [Keats's] painful life"[3]—marked by his reading of Spenser and Shakespeare as well as his discovery of his own poetic talents—his subsequent training at Guy's and St. Thomas's Hospitals, which he began when he was nineteen, exposed him to the horrors of early nineteenth-century surgery.

The medical students attended lectures on anatomy, physiology, and chemistry, but a major part of their curriculum required them to watch the doctors perform surgeries. The viewings took place in a claustrophobic amphitheater, where students crowded upon one another on the steep bleachers. The closeness of the quarters was nothing compared to the butchery of un-anesthetized patients. While stout assistants held the writhing, screaming victims down on the table, practitioners sawed off limbs, snipped off toes, sliced flesh, inserted forceps, broke bones for resetting, and stanched, the best they could, profuse bleeding. Even Astley Cooper, the age's most accomplished surgeon, veteran of hundreds of procedures, couldn't maintain his composure when he witnessed a child upon the table, unaware of what awaited him, smile. Cooper turned away and sobbed.[4]

Keats endured these scenes weekly, and actually got the worst of it, having been assigned to assist the most incompetent surgeon of the hospital, William Lucas, "rash in the extreme, cutting amongst the most important parts as though they were only skin."[5] Aside from stifling the cries of Lucas's unfortunate patients, sometimes by forcing the leather-wrapped cane between their teeth, Keats changed their bandages, and so daily faced fetid, pus-oozing wounds on gangrene's verge. He also set broken bones, pulled teeth, lanced boils, and performed, with leeches, "bleedings." He admitted and treated emergency patients. He might have delivered babies.

Clarke reported that Keats's despair during his time in the hospital was "irreversible," and George confessed that his brother was suicidal.[6] But Keats was resilient and competent. Despite his deadly depression, he thrived in the squalor and the blood. He was chosen to serve as a dresser only a month into his hospital training, an honor only 12 of a class of over 700 hundred received. He also passed the difficult apothecary quali-fication exam on his first try, a feat beyond many of his seemingly more diligent peers. This success gained him the official status of apothecary at the earliest possible age.

How did the dejected Keats triumph? He possessed a "vivid physical presence."[7] He was fiery (a "Fiery Particle," F. Scott Fitzgerald called him),[8] ready for a fight. Even when he was ill with consumption he fought a butcher for almost an hour after he saw the man torture a kitten. Keats won.

Keats's conviviality buoyed him as well. At Enfield, his impassioned shifts between "pugnacity and generosity" made him the most popular boy.[9] In the Borough, he exercised these winning traits. With his many friends from the hospital, he partook eagerly in the traditional plea-sures of early nineteenth-century men. He went to cockfights and boxing matches. He played billiards.

But the young Keats most solaced himself with the faculty that would soon become his enduring joy: his imagination. In a grisly environment where most would have raised cognitive defenses, Keats opened his mind, absorbed the tragedies, and translated them into vivacious art. His first great poem, "On First Looking into Chapman's Homer," exemplifies this alchemy.

✦

Clarke navigated the Borough's beastly turnings and knocked on his friend's door. As was their habit, he and Keats conversed about poetry. Soon, they lighted upon a book that had recently come into Clarke's pos-session, a 1616 folio of George Chapman's translation of Homer. Keats was keen on having a look. A few days later he arrived at Clarke's rooms and held the volume. The men began exchanging favorite passages.

Clarke later called the night one of the most "memorable" of his life. He was reading from book 5 of the *Odyssey*, in which Odysseus, after a shipwreck, emerges from the water, exhausted, with his "strong hands hanging down," "froth" on his "cheeks and nostrils flowing," feeling as though the "sea had soak'd his heart through." When Clarke looked up, he enjoyed the "reward of one of [Keats's] delighted stares."[10]

One reason Clarke remembered this animated countenance, was what issued: Keats's sonnet on reading Homer. At daybreak Keats walked back to Dean Street, two miles. Upon entering his room, he wrote. Within two hours he had completed his poem on the wonder of poetry, hesitating only once, to change the unintentionally comical phrase "low-brow'd Homer" to "deep-brow'd." He dispatched the sonnet to Clarke, who found it waiting on his breakfast table when he awakened at ten o'clock.

"On First Looking into Chapman's Homer" opens in the wispy realms of myth, charming and light, far from the gruesome Borough: "Much have I travell'd in the realms of gold, / And many goodly states and kingdoms seen." These regions evoke Arcadia, Eden, the Garden of the Hesperides, where golden apples grow.[11]

In the next two lines, the poet extends his fantastical travelogue. He has also been around "many western islands" that "bards in fealty to Apollo hold." These isles to the west summon the Fortunate Isles of Greek mythology, beyond the western sunset, blissful home of the heroic dead; and the Otherworld of Celtic lore, also a distant occidental island where deities, spirits, and dead worthies reside. The western islands in addition recall the more palpable Ithaca, west of the Greek mainland, where Homer places Odysseus, who actually, according to the legend Tennyson cites in his "Ulysses," tried to voyage, in old age, "beyond the sunset, and the baths / Of all the western stars." Keats's islands might refer, as well, to the Hebrides, often called the western islands. (Keats would visit these islands within two years, and delightedly stare at Staffa's weird basalt columns and the large sea cavern cleaving them.) These islands in the sonnet, wherever they are, accommodate bards who worship Apollo.

But lurking on the edges of these reveries, under them or farther west, are forces inescapable and grim, like the Borough. As Keats knew from *The Odyssey*, Hades lies in distant western seas. And the Celtic Otherworld is also sometimes envisioned as an underground kingdom of ghosts.

The escapist fancy always trails the sinister miasma from which it flees, and on which, tragically, it always, for its very existence, depends.

The next quatrain suggests that the poet is awakening to the rough sublunar textures from which moony dreams float. Actual people concern him. The first is Homer. He has heard of a "wide expanse" that "deep-brow'd Homer ruled as his demesne." This span is Homer's imaginative domain, in which his mind's Ithaca and Odysseus grow vividly alive, definitely more visceral, complex, and unique than the poet's hazy, clichéd fantasies. But the area is also the actual place where Homer the man dwelled. Though this region (as well as when Homer lived) is unknown, it did, and does, exist, tangibly. Keats's initial descriptor of Homer, "low-brow'd," hints that he was indeed picturing the poet in an earthy, perhaps coarse environment, dominated by sex and violence. Physical vigor fuels Homer's genius. The poet acknowledges as much when he claims that Homer is a *ruler* of a domain.

Poetic profundity is inseparable from physical baseness. Imaginative expansion requires a power-grab. The speaker confesses that he has been confused over the meaning of these ideas: he "never [could] judge what men could mean" when they spoke about Homer's demesne. But now Chapman has clarified. His "loud and bold" translation expresses the full force of Homer, his power and his knowledge, and the poet who earlier dabbled in fairy lore now awakens to the complex vitality of the verse.

The deepest meaning of Homer, for this poet, inheres not in the actual epics but in their influence upon him. Looking into Chapman, he feels like a "watcher of the skies" just at the instant a "new planet swims into his ken." An oceanic heaven dilates the mind but threatens to engulf it. This mixture of amplification and horror is sublime, as is the unfamiliar spheroid crossing into the astronomer's scope.

The poet switches similes, now identifies with "stout Cortez" at the instant he "with eagle eyes" stared "at the Pacific," and all of his men looked at "each other with a wild surmise— / Silent, upon a peak in Darien." Again an explorer pushes into waters, charts them. But bafflement remains, this time in Cortez's men, who stand stunned near the strange ocean, gawking not at the waves or their captain but at each other, unspeaking, speculating.

"On First Looking into Chapman's Homer" searches those galvanic instants, so rare, when we are most alive, most consumed by our immediate environment, intensely participatory. The experience is so profound we risk missing the meaning. We hover between awe and cogitation. The poet might suddenly apprehend Homer's depths, but the ecstatic comprehension is tenuous in a world of unceasing expansiveness.

There are different kinds of ignorance. One sort the poet exemplifies when he boasts of having traveled in folkloric realms. This is the benightedness of escapism. The poet grasps the superficiality of fantasizing when he turns to Homer, who exposes him to realities turbulent but also exhilarating. With his mists cleared, he wonders over the world's weird abundance. But by poem's end, he understands the earth's inscrutability. This second kind of unknowing, far from escapism, is sensitive to powers on the edge of awareness, that could at any instant float or lurch or leap into the light, altering everything.

✦

Soon after Keats completed "On First Looking into Chapman's Homer" in autumn 1816, Clarke introduced him to Leigh Hunt, the radical poet and editor. Hunt had earlier published Keats's anonymously submitted "O

Solitude!" in his newspaper, *The Examiner*. Upon learning from Clarke the identity of this promising young writer, Hunt arranged to meet him.

Clarke recalls Keats's thrilling first journey to Hunt, then living in Hampstead Heath: "The character and expression of Keats's features would arrest even the casual passenger in the street; and now they were wrought to a tone of animation that I could not but watch with interest. . . . As we approached the Heath, there was the rising and accelerated step, the gradual subsidence of all talk."[12] Hunt himself, on beholding the young poet minutes later, also noted the ardor, impressed by "the fine fervid countenance."[13] Immediately, Hunt, eleven years Keats's senior, more or less adopted the orphan (whom he soon affectionately called "Junkets"), setting up a bed for him in his cottage's library and encouraging him to visit anytime.

Hunt published some of Keats's other poems in *The Examiner* and wrote positively about them in an essay on "Young Poets," which praised Shelley as well. He also acquainted Keats with the painter Robert Benjamin Haydon, whose prodigious ambition awakened in Keats a craving for grand-scale glory.

In November, Keats composed a sonnet praising Hunt's and Haydon's ameliorative powers, as well as those of a poet he would soon meet, Wordsworth. These figures, the poem begins, are "Great Spirits . . . now on Earth sojourning." Their followers, now "standing apart / Upon the forehead of the Age to come," will revive the world, planting in it "another heart / And other pulses." Who else can hear, the sonnet asks, the "hum" of these "mighty Workings in the distant Mart?" Not many. The nations, the poem concludes, are "dumb"—speechless, but also ignorant before the immense wisdom of these three heroic spirits.

At the conclusion of the Homer sonnet, Cortez's men, on beholding the Pacific, are quiet, but awed. In this poem, those in earshot of the sublime triumvirate are mutely stupid. The mighty geniuses don't lift the masses but belittle them. Demeaned by greatness they will probably never understand or attain, those in the "distant Mart" are likely to lose their noble aspirations, loathe themselves, and resent those above them.

Just as Keats is finding his heroes, he reveals the dangers of hero worship: devotion to a great writer is as likely to paralyze as to inspire. Keats tottered on this line between striving and despair. Balancing became his art. To master the craft, he had to learn how to fall: successfully to fail.

Chapter 3

Sick Eagle

Haydon promised Keats that he would send this sonnet to Wordsworth, but the painter didn't deliver the verse for a month. Six weeks after receiving it, Wordsworth tepidly deemed the sonnet to be "of good promise."[1] He would convey a similarly lukewarm response toward the young man's poetry almost a year later, in December 1817, when Keats first met him in person.

The difference between the Keats of November 1816 and the one of December of the next year was radical. In critical acumen and poetic competence, he grew ten years, if not twenty, in the space of one. (But then each of the remaining four years of his brief life proved a vertiginous quickening of clock time.) His startling artistic progress was matched by his sheer physical dynamism—he switched dwellings eight times (ranging among several London neighborhoods, including Hampstead; the Isle of Wight, where his landlady gave him a portrait of Shakespeare; the coast of Kent; Oxford; and Stratford-upon-Avon, the Bard's birthplace)—as well as by his frantic socializing, which won him warm friendships with William Hazlitt, John Hamilton Reynolds, Charles Brown (a future travel companion and roommate), Benjamin Bailey, and Joseph Severn (who sketched the exhausted, fevered Keats only hours before the poet died in Rome).

Goading Keats was a decision he made on December 1, 1816: to drop his medical career, six years in the making and a guarantee of steady income, and become a full-time poet. The inheritance he had come into on October 31 of that year, handed down from his grandmother, had mostly been spent on his medical training, but enough remained, he thought, to supply him a small yearly income. He figured he would need to supplement his allowance with profits from his poetry. His guardian Abbey knew that Keats would make very little money, perhaps none at all, from versifying. He told John as much, and accused him of being "mad or a fool." Keats confidently retorted: "My mind is made up. I know that I possess Abilities greater than most Men, and therefore I am determined to gain my Living by exercising them."

Three months later, Keats seemed well on his way to the laurel. On March 3, his first book was published. He had high expectations for its success—for good reason. Hunt had enthusiastically supported the collection, called *Poems*, even arranging for his own publisher, Charles Ollier, to release it. The book contained the sonnet on Homer, widely praised, as well as two more recent poems Keats especially liked, "I stood tip-toe" and "Sleep and Poetry."

But the book barely sold at all and received almost no attention in the press. When Ollier lost interest in pushing the volume, George Keats asked in a brusque letter why the firm had let John down. Miffed, Ollier informed the younger brother that he was so weary of dissatisfied customers heaping "ridicule" upon the book that he was severing all connection with John Keats.[2]

Keats seemed stopped before he could get started, suffering at the outset of his publishing career a failure from which he might not recover. But just at the moment that his first book foundered, Keats, showing extraordinary resilience, didn't languish in self-pity or scold himself for publishing too soon. He boldly set for himself an even more ambitious poetic task, one whose possible failure would be far more damaging than the neglect of a first slight volume. Only days after *Poems* was published, he embarked on *Endymion*, an epic, a genre only Milton, among the English poets, had mastered.

How had Keats, so young and harried, so philosophically unseasoned and prone to mind-clouding melancholy, mustered the energy, seemingly perverse, to translate his faltering into a surge? In early March 1817, he stared delightedly at the Elgin Marbles, recently housed in the British Museum, and learned the grandeur of falling short.

✦

In January 2012 I visited these marbles with my wife Sandi and my ten-year-old daughter Una. I wanted to find the carved stones as moving as Keats did. The scenes to me seemed flat, though, and dull, and I was ashamed of my passion's dearth. I wanted to be the enthusiastic Keats, and all I could muster was Wilson at his worst: a man dead to beauty but nonetheless desiring nothing more than to be aesthetically alive.

I struggled with such moments often during my stay in London, paralyzed between apathy and self-loathing as I gaped at the earth's sublime productions. This mixture of indifference and indignation is depression at its most ruinous. Coleridge knew this. In "Dejection: An Ode," he describes "a grief without a pang, void, dark, and drear" that numbs him to scenes whose beauty he is nonetheless cursed to recognize.

Why was I depressed? You could say that my dejection arose from genes or circumstances or both, and you would almost certainly be right. But the truth of the matter, to me, based on my experience, seemed (and seems): depression—bifurcated in my case between dejection and mania—blows where it lists, often hits hardest when light is heightened. Unlike sadness or sorrow, which has a source in an actual event, depression has infected my good times and bad, has been worse, in fact, when everything's going my way. I enjoy a loving family, healthy body, successful career, exhilarating travel opportunities, good news galore, and I feel like killing myself.

Two months after we visited the Elgin Marbles—this would be March of 2012—Sandi, Una, and I visited the Keats House in Hampstead, near the Heath. On this day, I was even more sullen than I had been before the marbles, probably because of the exhausting pressure I put on myself to elevate to epiphany. Here, more than the museum, was my Mecca, akin in my mind to Thoreau's Walden Pond, where I had, when a younger pilgrim, gained insight into the sweet crossings of spirit and nature. (So I told myself.) I wanted a similarly meaningful experience in the rooms in which Keats had written the nightingale ode, fallen in love with Fanny, and suffered the consumption that would kill him in Rome. I wanted Una to enjoy an awakening as well, to the music of Keats's rhymes, or to the tale of his romance with Fanny.

Dante wrote that hell is the absence of hope. I humbly add: hell is the memory of hope's vitality coupled with the inability to enjoy it again. Lack without knowledge of the lacking: this hurts. But lack, locked-in lack, with keen awareness of the treasures missed: this is the slicing off of eyelids.

I'm at the Keats House. It's a palace of poetry, where the most marvelous thoughts were most musically managed. To imbibe its spirit, to stand and picture with gracious acuteness what happened on this bed, at this desk, in this sward of green, to picture these things and get "this is what it was like," and to feel this gone poet made new in my mind and veins, and, for once, to understand the essence of this creating man, to sense the joy of transcending the self into another more noble: to accomplish these welcome tasks—such would be worthy of this wondrous abode.

Unworthy, I looked at letters in Keats's own hand and saw only my disappointment over not making more of these precious pages. I gazed at volume 2 of Keats's very own copy of *Paradise Lost*, which inspired his monumental *Hyperion*; frustration clouded my eyes. I looked at a gilt bust of the poet, at the engagement ring he gave Fanny, at a lock of his hair contained within a medallion, and felt guilt.

Meanwhile, Una is bored and wants to leave. I tell her, "Let's go to the Heath."

We are making our way out. I light again on the green divan settled near a large front window. It opens onto the mulberry tree. The guide not twenty minutes earlier said that Keats, when his illness kept him from sleep, often requested that he be moved from his bedroom to this resting place; and I thought, vaguely, of how I once had a terrible fever when a boy, and my mom set me up on the couch in the living room so that I could watch TV. She hoped that the images would take my mind off my sickness. All day, I lay in a half-sleep infected with game-show talk and laugh-tracks.

Now, though, when I am only seconds away from exiting, the divan strikes me, like grace would a sinner, as a parable. I imagine the ailing Keats feeling isolated and claustrophobic in his small bedroom and wanting to be amidst others conversing in the window's light. I also see him sleeping out some nights on these cushions, awakened from his fitful, fevered slumber by a chorus of dawn birds. At those moments he thought, so I think to myself, "These creatures are the lovelier for my dying."

Sentimental, but I didn't care. This scene that I pictured recalled to me the transformation Keats perpetually achieved, through a combination of fortitude, imagination, and generosity. He converted his lacks, overwhelming—of parents, health, career success—into longings.

Bereft of those conditions most find essential for a contented life, Keats could easily have fallen into chronic depression, measuring all experiences by what they were not: affection from friends, not as good as a parent's love would have been; a nice walk on the Heath, not nearly as beautiful as it might be to a healthy man; a book of poems published—could have been so much better, and it received, to boot, bad reviews.

Keats chose against despair. He envisioned his orphaning as an invitation to love more intensely those who remained, his illness as a call to appreciate more keenly his rare good spirits, and his poetic limitations as a muse.

This is the conversion of depression into melancholy: sullenness over what's gone into yearning for what can come, apathy into somber hope, the limbo of mere lethargy, "no one thing is better than anything else," to the limbo of readiness: "everything, potentially, is interesting."

That's what melancholy, for Keats (now for me), is: not, again, depression, but a hunger for more life, so intense that the object longed for becomes more vivid than if possessed. C. S. Lewis used a German term to describe this pleasurable lacking, *Sehnsucht*, which means literally, "addicted to yearning," but defined by Lewis as "joy": the incompleteness forever generating rapturous images of completion. Or, as Lewis more felicitously put it: *Sehnsucht* is that "inconsolable longing" for "that unnameable something, desire for which pierces us like a rapier at the smell of bonfire, the sound of wild ducks flying overhead, the title of *The Well at the World's End*, the opening lines of 'Kubla Khan,' the morning cobwebs in late summer, or the noise of falling waves."[3]

As a stranger once said to me, during a conversation after I had given a lecture, Keats-inspired, on melancholy: "When we are born God scoops a hole in our soul, and we spend our lives trying to recover the sphere."

Keats on the divan: this was a man whose suffering bent his ear to the rounding and rounded notes of morning nightingales.

So I did have my vision that day after all, an "unnameable something" running through me. At least for that day, after stumbling into empathy over Keats on the divan, I labored to convert "no" to "yes." My daughter's boredom turned invitation for me to tell her the story of Keats getting into a fight over a kitten. My own failures before the Elgins and for the first nine-tenths of Hampstead: preparations for the insight I had now mercifully reached.

For *that* day: then soon the negating, like an addiction, returning, but at least now I had, and have, a kind of trick, the ability to gaze at the damp duck, de-focus, and see, just for a minute, the rabbit quick and bright—to see that ball of springing fur, and say, "OK," and that little two-syllable word morphs into a globe-shaped pebble that splashes into my murky waters and incites the concentric rippling.

✦

Keats did not need the goading I got. His response to the Elgin Marbles in the early spring of 1817 was immediately joyful, so much so that even his prodigious failures turned muted blisses. As was the case with his sonnet on Homer, Keats frantically composed a verse on the marbles only hours after beholding them, and put the completed poem in the hands of the friend who shared in the experience, in this case Haydon. Keats once more turned to the sonnet form and again focused on the power of sight.

The opening of "On Seeing the Elgin Marbles," however, differs radically from the beginning of the earlier sonnet. In place of a euphonic sentence redolent of Eden, is: "My spirit is too weak." Too weak for what? No answer, but more description of the poet's flagging spirit: "Mortality / Weighs heavily on me like unwilling sleep," he asserts, and "each imagin'd pinnacle and steep, / Of godlike hardship tells me I must die / Like a sick eagle looking at the sky." His death-destined body exhausts him into undesired slumber. Hypnogogic, he half imagines, half dreams Olympian peaks, accessible only to divine beings who can endure the terrible dangers and pains of the climb. These invented mountains intensify his infirmity, highlighting the gap between what he is and what he wants. He is like a once-majestic bird that knows the feeling of flight but is now grounded. The heavens taunt overhead.

This reverie of heights emphasizing his lowness is masochistic, a result of self-loathing. But the poet next strangely calls his partially self-induced despair a "gentle luxury": "Yet 'tis a gentle luxury to weep / That I have not the cloudy winds to keep / Fresh for the opening of the morning's eye." The syntax is odd, as if the poet really is drifting off to sleep. He might mean that he cries because he is not a god responsible for keeping the winds brisk for the sunrise. But he could also be suggesting that he weeps since no winds keep him fresh for the morning light.

Whatever he means, this poet sees himself as passive, lacking agency. The self-definition is the clue to why he prefers degrading fantasies to dawn awakenings, and why he considers his sorrow over these demeaning phantoms a luxury. He is certainly depressed, which is painful but also pleasurable, because the mood allows him to shirk responsibility. "I am depressed," this kind of thinking goes, "and so can't be expected to fulfill duties or obligations to myself or others. You wouldn't ask a man with tuberculosis to climb a mountain. Why would you ask a victim of depression—what I am—to undertake the labors of living: creating, loving, working? Leave me alone. Let me lie here."

In calling his lethargy a "gentle luxury," the poet emphasizes this perverse joy of his victimhood. However, in choosing one analysis of his condition over another—calling it a pleasure as opposed to pain, or something else—he transcends this same victimhood. He demonstrates an awareness of his role in creating his lowly state and so puts himself in a position of responsibility, in essence saying, "I believe that this is the reason for my weakness—I like it because it frees me from blame or praise—and am prepared to defend this argument." The poem, like the Homer sonnet, dramatizes a dull mind coming alive to its neglected powers.

The sestet develops this sensitivity. The poet confesses that his imaginings of treacherous mountains are "dim-conceived glories of the brain" that "bring round the heart an undescribable feud." His reveries are "dim" because they emerge from stupor, and "conceived" since they are mental phenomena. But they are glorious, too—conceptions as well as concepts: impregnations, leaps into life. Even though they sap energy and underscore inadequacy, these imaginings call forth, as do all obstacles, fresh powers and new creations, showing what he can't do now but might do later.

This duplicity of seemingly insurmountable obstacles sets the heart feuding with itself. Why is the battle "undescribable?" The poem thus far has done nothing *but* describe the feud. But the depictions, it appears, have failed. The rift is beyond verbal description. The ineffability, though, is not simply negative. "Undescribable" also connotes "too beautiful," "too transcendent." The feud is sublime: indefinable, frustrating to the meaning-seeking brain; but also euphoria inducing.

The poem next refers to the marbles for the first time: just as the "dim-conceived glories" cause vertigo in the heart, so these stone "wonders" produce a "dizzy pain." The imagined pinnacles and the conceptual glories and the marbles are synonymous. But the poet is most tormented and giddy over the stone, whose visceral proximity, only an arm-length away, sharpens the pain of his limitations while intensifying his ecstatic aspirations. The pressure pushes him to unprecedented concreteness: his bewildering agony arises from a mingling of "Grecian grandeur with the rude / Wasting of old time—with a billowy main, / A sun—a shadow of a magnitude."

Grecian art mixing with the flux of time: this is a paradox. The art participates in time, organizes it into more permanent structures; at the same time, the marbles are sucked into time's wastes, as liable to decay as daffodils. Both permanence and passing foment "dizzy pain." In transcending time, the marbles instill in the beholder pain over his decay and the joy of meditating on eternity. The carvings torment: nothing escapes annihilation; and uplift: earth generates exquisite artifacts.

This last insight prods the poet into new territory. For the first time in the poem, he acknowledges mortal beauties. Earlier, the sky, the "windy clouds," the "opening of the morning's eye," and the "sick eagle" were mere markers of his lack of vitality. Now, at poem's end, the physical world comes alive, valuable in its own right, clear of morose projections. The sea rises and plunges. The sun is the sun, and shines. A shadow extends from an immense presence.

Ironically, the poem concludes not with the marbles but with water, light, shadow. These ephemera pull everything inexorably toward death, but they also exuberantly undulate between gloom and glow. We need art to save us from mortality; we require nature to redeem us from artifice. The marbles, for all of their grandeur, are dead. Time's rude wastes, despite carnage, rouse.

The sonnet is about a poet becoming conscious of two kinds of failure: his failure to create immortal art, and the failure of art to provide lasting solace. Both sorts of faltering can result in despair: the torpor of giving up, or the devastation of a project botched.

But these failures are also muses: imperfections eliciting perpetual, creative pursuits of inaccessible finalities. For Keats, nothing but epic success will suffice, on the scale of Shakespeare. To aspire to this ideal is to guarantee defeat. The failure, though, generates consequential accomplishment.

Melville wrote that "it is better to fail in originality, than to succeed in imitation. He who has never failed somewhere, that man can not be great. Failure is the true test of greatness. And if it be said, that continual success is a proof that a man wisely knows his powers—it is only to be added, that, in that case, he knows them to be small."[4]

A poet can celebrate the faulty processes through which he nonetheless pictures perfection. He can also praise the inadequacy of his products, whose limitations point to the limitlessness they fall short of. Even his most finished works—even if they are the Elgins—can never approach the abundance, astonishing and inscrutable, of actual existence. To view these artifacts as revelations of what they are not is liberating, a transformation of their stasis into motion. Some works actually encourage this ironic reversal, highlighting their narrowness to urge audiences to fullness.

Melville again. In *Moby-Dick*, Ishmael says of Queequeg's home, "It is not down on any map; true places never are."[5] He thus emphasizes the gap between map and territory, text and world, and so suggests that the book he is writing is inadequate to the experience, whaling, the book is about. Indeed, Ishmael later admits that the "great Leviathan is that one creature in the world which must remain unpainted to the last." Still, though, Ishmael enthusiastically gestures toward the ineffable beast, encouraging readers to imagine it, with this hope: "one portrait may hit the mark much nearer than another."[6]

Chapter 4

Ethereal Chemical

What ensures that a portrait will fall well short of the event it wants to depict: hyper-fervid introspection, dwelling solely in "imagined pinnacles and steeps" and so severing attention from billows, lights, shadows. Such extreme inwardness is both an effect and cause of depression. To despair is to obsess over mental pain, lose interest in externals. This separation from the actual intensifies the inward gaze, and so widens the gap between inner and outer. The result is even more frantic Hamletizing.

That his strongest early sonnets describe the perils of navel-gazing suggests that the young Keats was well aware of his own imagination's severing powers. Although this faculty could generate poems opening toward the depths of experience—Pacifics and Elgins—it could also produce cogitations closing the senses down.

In the mind's dark shell imprisoned: this is another name for hell. Milton's Satan, from heaven hurled, wakes up bruised and burned in the "darkness visible."[1] He strains to convince himself that he still possess potency. He declares that his mind "is its own place, and in itself / Can make a Heaven of Hell, a Hell of Heaven."[2] He may be down, but he turns the world inside out.

When such mental power connects to the actual, poems originate. But when contact breaks, numbness results. Upon beholding Paradise and realizing that he can never defeat a God mighty enough to form such a bower, Satan understands: "Me miserable. Which way shall I fly / Infinite wrath, and infinite despair? / Which way I fly is Hell; myself am Hell."[3] Unable to escape his own mind, Satan can stare only at his own despair, no matter where he travels. He's doomed for all eternity to watch a film of his own making. Imprinted on every frame is an image of himself. The consummate hedonist is incapable of sensual enjoyment.

✦

Keats healthily feared his own inner imp, and endeavored to keep it occupied with vibrant sights and sounds. He knew not to recline overly long in the bowers of his brain. For every moment he brooded over imagination's makings, he relished the world's turbulence.

April 15, 1817. Keats stops in Southampton on his way to the Isle of Wight. He describes his journey to his brothers.

> I am safe at Southampton—after having ridden three stages outside and the rest in for it began to be very cold. I did not know the Names of any of the Towns I passed through—all I can tell you is that sometimes I saw dusty Hedges—sometimes Ponds—then nothing—then a little Wood with trees look you like Launce's Sister "as white as a Lilly and as small as a Wand"—then came houses which died away into a few straggling Barns—then came hedge trees aforesaid again. As the Lamplight crept along the following things were discovered— "long heath broom furze"—Hurdles here and there half a Mile—Park palings when the Windows of a House were always discovered by reflection—One Nymph of Fountain—*N.B. Stone*—lopped Trees— Cow ruminating—ditto Donkey—Man and Woman going gingerly along—William seeing his Sisters over the Heath—John waiting with a Lanthorn for his Mistress—Barber's Pole—Doctor's Shop— However after having had my fill of these I popped my Head out just as it began to Dawn.

This man sees with the vertiginous specificity of a hand-held Super 8. His phrases are brisk images; his dashes, the cuts.

April 17, 1817. Now settled at Carisbrook, on the Isle of Wight, Keats recounts to Reynolds his visit to Shanklin, a nearby village, the day before.

> [It] is a most beautiful place—sloping wood and meadow ground reaches round the Chine, which is a cleft between the Cliffs of the depth of nearly 300 feet at least. This cleft is filled with trees & bushes in the narrow parts; and as it widens becomes bare, if it were not for primroses on one side, which spread to the very verge of the Sea, and some fishermen's huts on the other, . . . perched midway in the Ballustrades of beautiful green Hedges along their steps down to the sands.—But the sea, Jack, the sea—the little waterfall—then the white cliff—then St. Catherine's Hill—"the sheep in the meadows, the cows in the corn."

Keats next turns to his current seaside abode.

I see Carisbrooke Castle from my window, and have found several delightful wood-alleys, and copses, and quick freshes—As for
Primroses—the Island ought to be called Primrose Island: that is,
if the nation of Cowslips agree thereto, of which there are diverse
Clans just beginning to lift up their heads . . . Another reason of
my fixing is that I am more in reach of the places around me—I
intend to walk over the Island east—West-North South—I have not
seen many specimens of Ruins—I dont think however I shall ever see
one to surpass Carisbrooke Castle. The trench is o'ergrown with the
smoothest turf, and the Walls with ivy—The Keep within side is one
Bower of ivy—a Colony of Jackdaws have been there many years.
I dare say I have seen many a descendant of some old cawer who
peeped through the Bars at Charles the first, when he was there in
Confinement.

✦

Three weeks after these exquisite pictures of grass, ivy, and jackdaws,
Keats is deep into *Endymion*, feeling, he confesses to Hunt, more confident than ever, having written every day for "about a Fortnight." But
the progress doesn't come easily, as he admits to his increasingly more
intimate friend Haydon. He fears that one unproductive day might begin
a longer period of "all sorts of irregularities." He is most afraid, however,
that his "horrid Morbidity of Temperament" will throw him into despair.
Shakespeare saves him from this descent.

Keats read Shakespeare intensely throughout the summer of 1817. The
plays, especially *King Lear*, eased his own worries as well as inspired him
to keep at his own writing. Shakespeare would continue to soothe Keats
for the rest of his life; more important to Keats, though, was Shakespeare
as exemplar of the empathetic poet, reconciling mental energy and alert
sensuality.

Overly active introspection seduces into solipsism. But compulsive
caressing of externals is equally troublesome, crowding the mind, stifling
contemplation and creativity. More dangerously, sympathizing or empa-
thizing too intimately with things outside the skin, one can lose identity,
become the environment, everything and nothing at once. Stare a long
time at the sea, your brain turns salty green-blue, sloshes to alien rhythms.

How to stand in the middle, between the mind's images and intensities
of matter—not too far, not overly close? Be Shakespeare, Man of Genius.

In a November 22, 1817 letter to Bailey, Keats tries to find this sweet
median. He laments the recent brusqueness of Haydon, attributes it to

arrogance. Then his mind turns to the man of genius: "In passing however I must say of one thing that has pressed upon me lately and encreased my Humility and capability of submission and that is this truth—Men of Genius are great as certain ethereal Chemicals operating on the Mass of neutral intellect—but they have not any individuality, any determined Character. I would call the top and head of those who have a proper self Men of Power."

Recalling his scientific studies, Keats imagines the genius's mind as a gaseous chemical that initiates a reaction in the neutral intellect of his audience. As a gas, the genius is mobile, expansive, porous, absorptive, passive, transformable—able to merge with, empathize with, other beings. But the ethereal mind is also active, potent, transformative, capable of changing the nature of those substances on which it operates, and so of altering the object with which it imaginatively merges. When involved in a chemical reaction, the gas catalyzes and is catalyzed: it converts the substance on which it acts into something else, just as it is converted into something other. The result: a new form. Oxygen reacts with iron: iron oxide. Analogously, the genius converts the minds of its audience into novel ways of seeing while being changed itself by imagining the audiences' thoughts and feelings. This interaction produces the artwork.

Keats's simile also explains the transformative alliance between the genius and his subject matter. If the genius's mind is a gaseous chemical, like oxygen, then the event to which the mind imaginatively attends is a substance on which the chemical acts, such as iron. The result of this blending is, once more, the poem, viewed this time from the perspective of artist and creation, as opposed to creation and audience. (Of course, what really makes a work of art is all three aspects working in concert: artist, creation, audience.)

After noting the opposite of the man of genius, the man of "Power," who holds tenaciously to his controlling ego, Keats explains how the genius becomes ethereal—through affectionate imagination. "I am certain of nothing but the holiness of the Heart's affections and the truth of Imagination—What the imagination seizes as Beauty must be truth—whether it existed before or not. . . . The imagination may be compared to Adam's dream—he awoke and found it truth." The poet empathizes most intensely with the events that he most loves. The love can be passion for beauty, compassion for those who suffer, regard for friends, devotion to the sacred, romantic endearment, erotic ardor. Whatever its nature, this affection is holy, because it is the source of transcendence (the self flowing out into another); intimacy (the self mingling with the other); beauty (the self appreciating the symmetries in the other); and, most importantly, truth.

Here Keats first connects imagination, truth, and beauty. The poet perceives an object that arouses his affection—a nightingale. He embraces it with his imagination, feeling what it is *to be* this thing outside his skin, seeing the world through its perspective, sensing the pressures surrounding it, sustaining it. This cognitive identification opens the poet to the aesthetic qualities of the object, its interactions between energy and form, power and meaning. So intense is this experience, so galvanizing, so palpably real, that the poet concludes that the encounter must be *true*. Keats doesn't mean truth with a big "T": truth as a law scientifically verifiable, a dictate handed down from heaven, or a statement airtight logically. Truth in this case refers to the authenticity of a particular moment, its electric actuality, its unmistakable significance—as in "This vision of the night bird happened; it shivered my nerves and my mind and animated into urgent import this instant of *being*."

Keats emphasizes this point—that truth generated by the apprehension of beauty is not purely objective—when he claims that the imagination can *create* truths that might not have before existed. Aesthetic truth arises from an interaction between poet and creature that has never been before, and will never be again. The creature is made new in this poet's unprecedented, passionate perception; the poet is freshly fashioned in the perspective of the unrepeatable, beloved creature. Adam dreams of a figure arousing his most ecstatic affection. When he wakes, Eve is there, a spring of fresh sensations and concepts. Truth for Keats is not simply subjective, either. The objects on which he imaginatively seizes are, like breathing Eve, actual, *there* for everyone to apprehend. The enduring reality of the physical world necessarily shapes the poet's imaginings, establishing what he can and cannot do. He can transform a nightingale into a marker of his longings, but he can't, if he wishes to address and heal the shared world, translate the bird, whimsically, into anything he wants. His objects can be subjectively inflected, but his subjectivity must be objectively realized.

Keats invites such philosophical terminology in the next section of his November letter to Bailey. He confesses that he is "more zealous" in his aesthetic convictions because he has "never yet been able to perceive how anything can be known for truth by consequitive reasoning—and yet it must be—Can it be that even the greatest philosopher ever arrived at his goal without putting aside numerous objections—However it may be, O for a Life of Sensation rather than of thoughts!" To remain logical, reason must ignore life's messy, vague, ephemeral, mysterious elements. In contrast to the rationalist, the poet is open to the weird myriadness of existence, the confusing as well as the lucid, insoluble darkness and light. The faculty most sensitive to duplicities and paradoxes, tortures and teachings, is not thought but sensation: physical and emotional contact. So vital is a life of sensation that Keats can only imagine an afterlife, a heaven, as a heightened version of earthly experience.

But Keats closes his letter coldly. "The world is full of troubles," he reminds himself and Bailey, and "Worldly Happiness" is most likely unattainable. If there is such a thing as happiness, it comes in those flashes in "the present hour": the sun, the sparrow.

Neither feather nor beam reconciles Keats to his lot just now. He has been in a funk for the past week, unable to "feel" the "influence of a passion or affection." This lethargy might appear to Bailey to be "heartlessness" but it is in fact "abstraction," the inability to generate the concrete sensations that make life worth living. When Keats descends into such depressed moods, he begins to "suspect" himself and the "genuineness of [his] feelings at other times—thinking them a few barren Tragedy tears."

Chapter 5

✦

Negative Capability

Sensation is truth. Don't trust the senses. Are both statements valid? Maybe Keats in this letter to Bailey is saying no, one or the other is true, but he just doesn't know which. Or perhaps he is suggesting that mood dictates apparent veracity—in a good mood, life appears to be one way, in a somber temper, another. But Keats might be implying that, regardless of confusion or shifts in perspective, life is irreducibly, intractably double, and the poet, if he is to be potent, salubrious, Shakespearean, must reconcile to this difficult fact and translate it into art.

Keats isn't ready to address this challenge in his poetry. Only six days after writing the letter, he finishes *Endymion*, a Platonic allegory in which the hero aspires to an empyrean purely sweet and light. Absent are Shakespeare's more complex explorations of crepuscular time.

The first lines, too famous to quote, but too beautiful not to, establish the ideal Endymion is seeking. "A thing of beauty is a joy forever: / Its loveliness increases; it will never / Pass into nothingness." Rather, it "still will keep / A bower quiet for us, and a sleep / Full of sweet dreams, and health, and quiet breathing."

An eternal green enclosure, holy Eden: this is what beauty is. Even if this beauty animates actual pastures, sun and moon, sheep and daffodils, musk roses and clear streams, it ultimately transcends the flux, as heaven hovers over earth.

Endymion pines to rise from earth to heaven. Though he dwells regally in the delicious climes of Latmos, he harbors a "lurking trouble." This unease separates him from his tranquil community of well-proportioned shepherds and shepherdesses, who worship Pan's natural cycles, which ensure that death is but preparation for new life, and somberness, for beauty more refined.

Endymion confesses to his sister Peona the cause of his vexations. In a dream in which he was studying the stars, he fell into an "airy trance," and soon found his soul commingled with the "argent spheres" of the moon. He then saw a beautiful, golden-haired woman. She pressed his hand, and away they flew. Ecstatic, aroused, Endymion in this dream within his dream madly kissed her. They then descended to a mountain meadow. He awakened from both fantasies. Overcome by melancholy yearning for his lunar consort, he found the earth, formerly gorgeous, a filthy prison, and still does.

Peona chastises him for sorrowing over a mere dream, but Endymion defends his "ardent listlessness" with an encomium to all quests for "fellowship divine." Happiness, he claims, does not lie in the "world's praises" but in the power that "becks / Our ready minds" to merge with "essence," until we "shine, / Full alchemized, and free of space." The first step in this ascent marks our elevation from raw facts into emotional or mental forms—the sound of wind into music, for instance. Superior to this level is human friendship, which approaches the "chief intensity" of communing with another person. But love reaches the goal. The influence of this "orbed drop / Of light" melts us into the "radiance" of the beloved. As fine as this mortal love is, however, it is not the very highest state: immortal love is, now consuming Endymion.

This speech concludes book 1. For the remaining three books, Endymion quests for his beloved. The journey is allegorical, the decaying mortal in search of immortal beauty. Like Cupid's lover Psyche, to whom Keats will later dedicate an ode, Endymion must prove worthy of his spiritual amour, who is the moon goddess herself, Cynthia.

He toils through the underworld, the sea, and the heavens. But just as he is on the verge of uniting with the divinity, he sees an Indian Maiden and falls passionately in love. He is now "cut" between this Maid and the goddess. While he is wavering, he dreams of his heavenly beloved, who first reveals her identity. Endymion nonetheless chooses the Maid. He will abandon his spiritual quest and dwell once more in Pan's realm, hopefully with her. No. She is forbidden to him.

Peona appears, and Endymion woefully says he will turn hermit. Before he renounces the world, however, he will visit Cynthia's temple one more time. There he finds the Indian Maid and Peona. The Maid transforms into Cynthia, who had simply taken on this earthly form. Endymion and Cynthia vanish "far away," leaving Peona to wander "[h]ome through the gloomy wood in wonderment."

✦

What began as an allegory of a mortal's quest for eternal beauty dissolves into a muddle. Given Endymion's progress from underworld to air, we expect him to move steadily in the poem's final book to his desired union. That he falls in love with a woman of this earth in only seconds is odd. That he chooses this mortal maiden over his goddess after he beholds the deity in her full luminousness: this is even stranger. But the most bizarre of all is that Cynthia herself would become a mortal in order to test her lover's devotion, then witness him fail the test miserably, and next grant him his reward anyway, union with her. The quickness with which this last event occurs only adds to the weirdness: about twenty-five lines. No wonder poor Peona wonders off alone into the dark forest.

Is the Maiden real, or a phantom of the goddess? Is the goddess herself, who reveals herself to Endymion in dreams, entirely actual? Which is better, spirit manifested in matter, or spirit untrammeled by earth? Perhaps realizing that *Endymion* ends in this confusion over what's authentic and what isn't, Keats admits in his preface that the poem is not a "deed accomplished" but a "feverish attempt," most of which is unworthy of "passing the press."

But if these allegorical perplexities thwart the Platonic moral, they illuminate Keats's development as a thinker during the composition of the poem. In fact, these textual agitations show a conflict between two competing Bildungsromans: the one of Endymion, rising from matter before getting mired in a metaphysical muddle; and the one of Endymion's creator, Keats, which sinks into matter's muck and sloshes around.

"Muddle," for E. M. Forster, is a philosophical term. Forster's characters—such as Lucy Honeychurch in *A Room with a View*—often find themselves in cognitive messes. They don't know what they need to thrive, and what they think they require worsens their plight. The characters who flourish—like Lucy—abide the muddle, and in their refusal to leap to old certainties, gain new understanding, which arises, ironically, not from knowing more, but less. As Zadie Smith writes, in "growing less 'certain,' less morally enthusiastic," Forster's characters move "closer to the good [they are] barely aware of desiring."[1]

Forster's explorations of muddles, Smith notes, owe much to the writer whose letters he was reading while composing *A Room with a View*: John Keats. For Forster, Keats had "seized upon the supreme fact of human nature, the very small amount of good in it, and the supreme importance of that little." This fact is the value of "Negative Capability," the deliberate willingness to remain in uncertainty.

Smith calls this Keats's "positive ethical strategy": turning a muddle, by enduring it without bitterness, meaningful, and ultimately beneficial, ignorance intensifying to knowledge. If a negatively capable muddle is an ethical stance, then is there such a thing as "unethical" muddle? Yes, if we call "unethical," "unproductive." One could find oneself in a muddle, know it, but instead of working through it flee to old dogmas. Or, one could be in a muddle and be mostly unaware of it, feeling uneasy, confused, or sorrowful, or all at once, and not know why. A person could actually fall into a muddle in the middle of these two reactions. He could be vaguely aware that something's not quite right, and vacillate between certainties and perplexities.

Endymion in book 4, his heart cloven between earth and heaven, is in a muddle. But he doesn't endure the confusion long enough to gain insights on the complicated, potentially rich relationships between the actual and the ideal. Instead, quickly wearied of the rift, he pushes toward the hermitage.

Keats, the hero's creator, is likewise in a muddle, and just as unproductive. He begins his epic confidently enough as an allegory of the quest for eternal beauty, but ends in confusion, unsure if the ideal is more valuable than the actual. Certainly, this kind of shift could make for enlightening poetry, like the great odes Keats will later write, which deliberately explore the terrible, vitalizing duplicity of being alive. But this luminousness is lacking in *Endymion*, because Keats doesn't, Virgil-like, guide us into the dim interstices. As he appears in the poem, as narrator and occasional commentator on the verse, he seems just as unaware as Endymion of the fecundity of bafflement.

✦

Unlike the youthful Keats who composed *Endymion*, I, much older, have been *aware* of the potential fruitfulness of confusion, but that knowledge has almost never done me any good. I have been afraid.

Nothing, for me, has been easier than believing in the value of elasticity. Ever since I first loved poetry—in the early days of college, when I was the age of the *Endymion*-composing Keats—I have most enjoyed writers committed to expansiveness, flexibility, playfulness, indeterminacy, inscrutability. These poets have become my livelihood and my life: Blake, Wordsworth, of course Keats, Whitman, and Dickinson.

The affection has been constitutional. Not for an instant was I drawn to Victorian lamenters over lost orders, the versifiers of the Age of Reason, the Renaissance micro-macro composers, or medieval allegorists. I lacked the seriousness or rectitude required to enjoy such writers. I also possessed—and this a blessing—an ironic sense of humor, early favoring Steve Martin and Bill Murray, while finding the more obvious sitcomish comedians—the Cosbys and the Roseannes—unfunny.

The poetic precisely was *capaciousness*, the ability to be two, six, a multitude of things at once, all the while aware of the manifoldness, reveling in its fecundity.

What I serenely espoused in theory, proved impossible in practice. Though I based a successful student and then academic career on the fruits of negative capability, in my non-bookish life I was obsessive, controlling, closed.

By the age of thirty-five, I had reduced my life to the workaholic's rigid routine. (I now realize that my labor obsession issued from the manic side of my depression.) Get up 4:30 every morning; write almost 500 words on the latest scholarly project; run six miles, same route; go into the office, write another 250; read, research, teach; come home at 5:00, drink two martinis, one beer with dinner, one scotch after; watch a film on DVD; go to bed; start over.

I was afraid of the insecurity I praised in prose. I feared that if I softened for a second, it would not be exhilarating flux on which I would ride, but rather I would mire into depression's cold muck. My routine, though static as all machine-like processes are, at least gave me the illusion of progression.

Una, born in 2002, blasted my engines. She came crying into the air and light, requiring for her survival that I compromise my habits. I traded writing for rocking, training for feeding, booze for coffee. Stripped of my props, I fell heavily depressed. Everything from tying my shoes to cooing with Una felt worthless. I vacillated between not caring that I didn't care, and worrying over how my apathy was harming my child.

What I was missing was the middle: either chaos for me, or order. I knew that such crass dualism enervates. It reduces multitudinous existence to twoness, impoverishing possibility, before striving for merely the one: the world as the beloved antinomy alone, with the other annihilated—order vanquishing chaos, turbulence overwhelming all reason.

The tragedies of so many characters stem from this severing. Lear must have either full fealty or none at all. Ahab holds that the world must be either totally meaningful, with each event serving as a symbol in a cosmic volume, or utterly insignificant, whales and everything else, ciphers simply.

How could such hierarchical cleaving result in anything other than pained solitude, sullen retreat into the cramped cave of one's own monomania? Lear may rave in the widest wild, and Ahab struggle among oceans un-soundable, but both might as well be hunched over in small darkness, dreaming of themselves dreaming of themselves.

The furies of a Lear or an Ahab cover cowardice. Both men fear loving and being loved, conditions requiring vulnerability, forgiveness, dependency, emotional and intellectual insecurity. Striving though you gave away your crown to rule all, fighting the most malicious leviathan—these are nothing compared to opening generously to another, navigating the middle ground between "I" and "thou," mustering in this median imagination, empathy, self-effacement, humor, art.

Keats bravely explored this mysterious mean. His example nudged me toward the redemptive middle, around the time Una turned three.

While rereading Bates's masterful biography of Keats, I noticed the poet perpetually translating his insights into *action*. No gap between being and knowing hounded him. The potential for doing was the precondition of apprehension. When he lighted upon negative capability, he became negatively capable. He understood in Shakespeare only what he needed to be a better poet. He minded his body, embodied his mind.

I decided to copy the visceral Keats. Reading a whole book for the sake of finishing it, cogitating to the end of a theory—I rejected such as escapism, art too far from life. Read as you would eat; once nourished, leave the table.

Keats freed me from plate-cleaning. He made me fit. I began to know newly, asking not, "what does it mean?," but "what does it do?"

I turned from bookworm to survivalist. I read unsystematically, driven only by one requirement: it must inspire. Half-perused books, from Berryman's *Dream Songs* to a biography of Faraday, lay spread open and upside down, on my floor, on my desk.

More importantly, Keats's pragmatism liberated how I interpret the narrative of my own life. I no longer try for synoptic accuracy. I focus now on those instances, rare, in which I don't feel one way or the other, morose or manic. Emphasizing these more ambiguous moments—like feeding Una from a jar while absent-mindedly watching *Sesame Street*, or teaching irony in Byron's *Don Juan*, or walking out one sunny morning after an ice storm, when the world shines—loosens my depression.

My mental illness is not synonymous with my being. I'm not *either* manic *or* sullen, and nothing else. Experiences outside these categories shape me just as much as those encounters within. Just as I can trade "I'm a scholar" for "I read to live," I can exchange "I am depressed" with "I have depression."

From new knowing, springs doing. More imaginative fatherhood, for instance, neither grim nor anxious: staging surreal plays with Una, with my character a pompous Lucifer, hers a self-righteous angelic bear; or arranging drawing games, in which each of us draws a crazy scribble, out of which the other must make a saner image.

The extremes still seduce, and sometimes I weaken. But even during my most forceful reversions to the old dualism, I know I am not simply continuous with the poles. There is more to me, muddled and possible.

✦

The great shift in Keats's poetic career occurred when he learned the difference between unproductive and productive muddles. While he labored to bring *Endymion* to a close, he was becoming engrossed in sensual experiences that turned spirit dreams anemic. In the summer of 1817, he frequently roused himself from "his fits of seeming gloomful reverie" by walking with his friend Severn out into Hampstead Heath. There he "would stand, leaning forward, listening intently, watching with a bright serene look in his eyes and sometimes with a slight smile, the tumultuous passage of the wind above the grain. The sea, or thought-compelling images of the sea, always seemed to restore him to happy calm."[2] Such sensitive and solacing encounters—much more intense than those experiences of jackdaws during the Isle of Wight spring—grew increasingly common for the maturing Keats. "Nothing seemed to escape him, the song of a bird and the undernote of response from covert or hedge, the rustle of some animal, the changing of the green and brown lights and furtive shadows . . . even the features and gestures of passing tramps, the colour of one woman's hair, the smile on a child's face."[3]

Keats was more and more realizing that such empathy produces productive muddles, out of which can cohere the most powerful poetry. To empathize with existence, as Shakespeare did, is to find oneself riven, pulled multitudinous directions, sensing in quick succession or all at once, a mollusk's slime, time's abysm, an ensign's psychopathy, the madness of an old king. Such mixings require that one have not just double vision, but triple, quadruple, more—a veritable peacock quantity. And with each vision comes emotions, ideas, often blended, blurred—dejection, joy, doubt, striving, malaise, anxiety, rage, readiness, certainty, resignation.

By December 21, 1817, hovering between *Endymion*'s things forever beautiful and the ripples of meadow grass, Keats finds language, lacking in his long poem, for this prolific poly-vision. Essential to the fruitful muddle is *intensity*, which Keats develops in the same letter in which he first defines negative capability

In the letter, Keats mentions his recent viewing of Benjamin West's *Death on a Pale Horse*. The apocalyptic painting struck him as "wonderful," but he found in it "nothing to be intense upon; no woman one feels mad to kiss, no face swelling into reality." Intensity, he insists, is "the excellence of every art," and this intensity is not simply the depiction of presences so compelling that they seem fascinatingly alive. Intensity is also present in art where "all disagreeables evaporate" because they are "in close relationship with Beauty and Truth." *King Lear* exemplifies this combination of force and agreeability: unlike West's painting, which represents "unpleasantness" without exciting "momentous depth of speculation," the Shakespeare tragedy unflinchingly reveals what is most repulsive about existence but elevates the ugliness to aesthetic and philosophic richness.

Keats gleaned his vision of intensity from Hazlitt's 1816 "On Gusto," in which the essayist describes this quality in a Titian. The painting, which features Acteon hunting, has "a brown, mellow, autumnal look," with the "sky . . . the colour of stone," and the "winds . . . sing[ing] through the rustling branches of the trees." So alive is the scene that one might hear upon beholding it "the twanging of bows resound through the tangled mazes of the wood." The work, Hazlitt asserts, is typical Titian. All of the artist's heads "seem to think—his bodies seem to feel." Indeed, the flesh "seems sensitive and alive all over; not merely to have the look and texture of flesh, but the feeling in itself." In general, Titian's images are "absolute, unimpaired, stamped with all the truth of passion, the pride of the eye, and the charm of beauty." This gusto, Hazlitt adds, gives Shakespeare's "dramatic invention" its "infinite quantity."[4]

Hazlitt's gusto, Keats's intensity: these terms signify the ineffable aliveness in great works of art—we want to touch them—as well as their profound meaning—they inspire new, enlarging ideas, or old ones refreshed, resized. Most works tilt to one side or the other, to verisimilitude or concept. For Keats, West's painting of death goes too far toward idea: "wonder." Hazlitt finds the same to be true of Claude's landscapes. They are too accurate, resembling "a mirror or microscope."[5]

Lear combines precision and energy. It limns suffering and evil with nightmarish specificity. The mad king's agony, eye's vile jelly, forked animals: these rivet the senses. But the scenes stimulate our minds as well, producing frameworks in which the suffering is meaningful. Blending truth—unadorned existence, inscrutable and luminous—and beauty—compelling affirmation of life as a never-expiring invitation to imagine and interpret—*Lear*, like all powerful art, exemplifies the "tragic gaiety" of Nietzsche: one ascends joy's height only by encompassing the *whole* of life, Dionysian chaos as well as Apollonian order.

In his December 21 letter, Keats next shows how to achieve intensity. He mentions a recent social gathering where sharp wit was on display. It occurs to him that wit simply makes one "start," surprises one, "without making one feel." It is really no more than a "mannerism," similar to table etiquette. By contrast, humor, "superior" to wit, is a more robust form of comedy, funniness with affect: the belly laugh, not the chuckle.

This distinction leads to another, between dogmatism, the "wit" of the philosophical realm, and flexibility, philosophy's humor. Philosophical wit is "disquisition," overly formal, removed from the unpredictable shifts of actual thinking. The humor of philosophy is "dispute": improvisation, openness, exuberance.

After a disquisition, not a dispute, with Dilke (who needed, Keats observed, to make "up his Mind about every thing" before he could feel "personal identity"), "several things dove-tailed in [Keats's] mind, and at once it struck [him]" what quality creates a genius like Shakespeare. This quality eludes the didactic Dilke, the dinner wits, and West; and it entails conversation, humor, Titian. It is negative capability: "when a man is capable of being in uncertainties, Mysteries, doubts, without any irritable reaching after fact & reason." Foregoing cognitive security prepares the poet to empathize with the muddled world, to embrace while transforming to beauty its inscrutable truths.

Take this analogy between reality and gravity. Gravity presses each of us down to the bottom. The negatively capable poet, intense, wants to feel gravity at its greatest. He leaps from cliffs into oceans. He will smack the water. But he jackknifes, flips, spins, or reaches into a swan. The disagreeable, being flung forcefully down, vanishes, with the hush of the faint splash. The cliché refreshed: poetry in motion.

Chapter 6

✦

Disinterestedness

From October 1816, when he wrote his sonnet on Chapman, to December 1817, the month he conceived negative capability, Keats had progressed from an obscure surgeon's assistant stuck in the Borough into a well-published poet living in Hampstead's meadows, where he mingled with Hunt, Haydon, Hazlitt, and Wordsworth. In fact, as though his life were an allegory, with well-planned markers of his most significant advancements, his first great artistic year was punctuated by the so-called Immortal Dinner, held in Haydon's house on December 28. Keats reveled with Wordsworth and Lamb, among others, including the explorer Joseph Ritchie, who promised Keats that he would carry a copy of *Endymion* into Egypt, and "fling the [it] in the midst of the Sahara."[1] (If he did, we don't know; he died on his African expedition only a year later, in Timbuktu.)

Keats's poetic development was just as rapid as his rising among the literati. A little over a year before this heroic party, Keats was tinkering with frilly paeans to Greek deities. Now he was fashioning brilliant letters and evolving a new style: "a more naked and Grecian manner," far from the "deep and sentimental cast" of *Endymion*.

Keats's early winter enthusiasm quickly died, though: in January, he had to nurse his brother Tom, whose health was deteriorating rapidly, and so had little time or energy for poetry. He was also putting up with a petty squabble among his closest friends, as well as a terrible depression.

But if Keats gained little poetic traction during this spring of 1818—producing only a conventional romance, *Isabella, or the Poet of Basil*, one notable sonnet, and some short, minor pieces—he did nonetheless continue to burgeon, prodigiously, as a thinker. His letters of this time profoundly meditate on the poet's proper ethics.

In his third letter of the year, addressed to his brothers and completed on January 19, he confesses that he is "quite perplexed in a world of doubts & fancies—there is nothing stable in the world—uproar's your only musick." The impetus for this confusion is a petty "quarrel of a severe nature between Haydon & Reynolds & another . . . between Hunt & Haydon." Keats is thankful for Bailey, who refuses to sink to childish squabbling. He exemplifies "probity & disinterestedness," qualities at the "tip top of any spiritual honors."

This is Keats's first significant mention of "disinterestedness," his highest ethical and poetical standard. He gathered it from Hazlitt, whose *Essays on the Principles of Human Action* explores the "Natural Disinterestedness of the Human Mind." Hazlitt argues that empathy is the mind's primary epistemological mechanism. In order to know anything, even myself, I must employ sensation, memory, and imagination. I learn the relationships between myself and the world through sensory data—a nectarine tastes good, the briar hurts. These experiences give me my sense of self—"I am he who feels this way or that." I require memory to remind myself that it was I who felt these things in the past, but I need imagination to picture myself as this same identity in the future. For Hazlitt, this envisioning of the future of my identity requires empathy, the ability to transcend my position in the present and identify with my being in the future. Self-love necessitates "other-love."[2]

Future-orientated imagination also enables us to identify with beings outside our skin. "Selfless" love of self leads to egoless love of others. We empathize most forcefully with the beings toward which we have the strongest feelings, and in identifying with them, mimic them. We wince when we see another in pain, or we cry when another is sad. The longer we experience these beings, the more closely we imitate them, the better we know them. This increase in knowledge in turn deepens our empathy, which increases our knowledge, and so on. Disinterestedness is required for interest. Egolessness is necessary for the self's striving. Shakespeare, the greatest man, was "was nothing in himself; but . . . all that others were, or that they could become. . . . He had only to think of anything to become that thing."[3]

Keats wrote Bailey his disinterested friend only four days after completing his January 19 letter. His friends' feuds still vex. He pleads for tolerance: "Men should bear with each other—there lives not the man who may not be cut up, aye hashed to pieces on his weakest side. The best of Men have but a portion of good in them—a kind of spiritual yeast in their frames which creates the ferment of existence—by which a Man is propell'd to act and strive and buffet with Circumstance." The way to realize this generosity is "first to know a Man's faults, and then be passive, if after that he insensibly draws you towards him then you have no Power to break the link." Before he "felt interested in either Reynolds or

Haydon," he was "well read in their faults." He nonetheless still has been "cementing gradually with both."

To know a man's faults fully, one must become passive before them, accept him, identify with him, empathize with him. Our shared weaknesses (there is no one who can't be "hashed to pieces on his weakest side") enable us to do this. Common inadequacy is friendship's unbreakable bond. Seeing the worst in oneself is recognizing the best in others.

Keats equated the principles of good friendship with those of good writing: both require egolessness. He develops this connection in a January 25 letter to his brothers, where he reports a squabble of his own. Hunt and Shelley are both "hurt & perhaps justly, at [his] not having showed them" *Endymion* before submitting it to the printer. He withheld the work because "they appear much disposed to dissect & anatomize, any trip or slip I may have made." But unlike the hot-tempered Haydon, Keats is humble enough to admit that he might have been wrong. He acknowledges that Hunt and Shelley probably really wanted to help him, but he was too insecure to take their criticisms.

He then suggests the cause of his insecurity: his fear of conflict. Now overcoming this aversion, he is ready to face hard problems, and has written a sonnet on *King Lear* to commemorate his commitment. He bids farewell to "golden tongued Romance" and embraces "the fierce dispute, / Betwixt Hell torment & impassioned Clay." ("Hell torment" becomes "damnation" in the sonnet's final version.) This trading of the "serene Lute" for the "bitter sweet of this Shakespearean fruit" will make him a better companion and poet.

After quoting the sonnet, Keats shifts to a mode that will increasingly energize his letters: comedy. A few days earlier, he attended a private theatrical of the "lowest order, all greasy & oily, insomuch that if they had lived in olden times, when signs were hung over the doors; the only appropriate one for that oily place would have been—a guttered Candle." Unimpressed by this oily crew, he and his friends forgo watching most of the performance, but return just before the show ends and enter, on a lark, the green room. There he finds a ludicrous assortment of actors worthy of Bottom and his crew. There is first a "painted Trollop." She is frustrated over her failure to play the virgin Mary well, and exclaims, "'damned if she'd play a serious part again, as long as she lived.'" This outburst causes a quarrel among the players, quieted when "a fat good natured looking girl in soldiers Clothes" says that she wishes she were a man. Then a man breaks into song "but an unlucky finger-point from the Gallery sent him off like a shot." Keats notices another "dressed to kill for the King"; he is standing at the edge of the stage "in the very sweat of anxiety to show himself." He never makes his scene, though, because the "musicians began pegging & fagging away at an overture—never did you see faces more in earnest, three times did they play it over, dropping all kinds of correctness."

To take pleasure in the ridiculous is typical of Keats's humor. He has an eye for the absurd and concocts an appropriately hyperbolic style. The jokes are never acerbic or cruel; instead they rely on bemused mockery—always at a harmless distance from those mocked. This comedy is "Shakespearean," taking joy in the silliness of pomp. Such humor calls attention more to the zaniness of life than to the wit of the one joking. It is negatively capable: observing the world as it risibly is.

Keats returns to this relationship among comedy, poetics, and friend-ship two weeks later, in a letter to Reynolds. He questions the received wisdom that one should read one's poetic contemporaries. Though he admits that some of his peers have produced some fine poetry, he crit-icizes their tendency to press a "palpable design" upon readers, when proper poetry "should be great & unobtrusive, a thing which enters into one's soul, and does not startle it or amaze it with itself but with its sub-ject." But these general remarks disguise Keats's probable intention, to say to Reynolds, still stuck in a grudge match with Haydon: let go of your own dogmas.

Keats then mocks narcissistic poets by comparing them to flowers that would "lose their beauty were they to throng into the highway crying out, 'admire me I am a violet! dote upon me I am a primrose!'" He con-tinues in the comic vein: such poets are like "an Elector of Hanover" who "governs his petty state, & knows how many straws are swept daily from the Causeways in all his dominions & has a continual itching that all the Housewives should have their coppers well scoured."

Keats hopes to avoid this petty self-regard—especially present in Wordsworth and Hunt—by imitating the Elizabethans, who presented the world as they saw it, careful not to reduce it to a reflection of their egos. He then exemplifies his own open-mindedness by admitting that he might have a limited view of Hunt and Wordsworth. Wordsworth exudes "grandeur," and Hunt possesses "merit." The men are complicated, and it would be unimaginative to flatten them to one quality.

Keats relates poetry, ethics, and comedy in another post to Reynolds, on February 19. He describes the pleasure of indolence: "When a Man has arrived at a certain ripeness in intellect any one grand and spiritual passage serves him as a starting point towards 'the two-and thirty Pal-laces.' How happy is such a 'voyage of conception,' what delicious diligent Indolence!" This lassitude is not laziness; it is negative capability, akin to

Whitman's "loafing" in "Song of Myself," where the American poet deliberately withholds himself from committing to one purpose or another, so
that he can be prepared for experiences that might expand his soul.

Keats's indolence is active imagining. "A nap upon the Clover engen-
ders ethereal finger-pointings—the prattle of the child gives it wings, and
the converse of middle age a strength to beat them—a strain of musick
conducts to 'an odd angle of the Isle' and when the leaves whisper it
puts a 'girdle round the earth.'" To doze in this mood is to become Puck
rushing round the earth. Such dynamic poeticizing translates to powerful
knowledge, much more potent than the information memory provides.
One should resist retrospection and project his mind forward—like the
spider, who begins her web-work from a few "points of leaves and twigs"
but soon "fills the Air with a beautiful circuiting," an "airy Citadel" spun
from her "own inwards." This wispy architecture then stays still, waiting
for the nourishment the future might bring. When a man engages in this
arachnid behavior, he is "content with as few points to tip with the fine
Webb of his Soul and weave a tapestry empyrean—full of Symbols for his
spiritual eye, of softness for his spiritual touch, of space for his wandering
of distinctness for his Luxury."

Touch life lightly, making as few permanent connections as possible.
From this initial network, express your thoughts and feelings unobtru-
sively, weaving a fine gossamer worldview, your own text. Then let the
web do its work, active and passive at once—take in new, nourishing
experiences that alter, while being changed by, the weave.

Keats turns this metaphor for the negatively capable mind to the ethics
of human interaction. If we could conceive of our minds as sensitive webs,
then our mental networks "would leave each other in contrary directions,
traverse each other in Numberless points, and all [at] last greet each other
at the Journeys end." A rewarding human relationship is an interweaving of different networks—first enmeshing at this point, then that, then
pulling away, only to interlace at another knot, and finally to recover
the initial braiding. In such a relationship, an old man and child could
learn from each other. Though the elderly fellow has more experience and
wisdom than the child, he is willing to explore the child's way; although
the child is limited in his knowledge and unaware of the extent of his
limitations, he is also ready to think about things from the older man's
perspective. To foster such elegant, mutually enlightening interchanges,
we should "whisper results" to our neighbors—humbly, respectfully.
Then "every human might become great, and Humanity instead of being
a wide heath of Furse and Briars with here and there a remote Oak or
Pine, would become a grand democracy of Forest Trees."

We should be like spiders. We should be like flowers, too, not bees. Bees are always "hurrying about and collecting," impatient for a "knowledge of what is to be arrived at." Zealous for future reward, they neglect the beauty of the present moment. The flower, attuned to the present, enjoys a more fruitful existence. It is "passive and receptive—budding patiently under the eye of Apollo and taking hints from every noble insect that favors [it] with a visit." If we would foster our floral nature, we would drink sweet dew.

Keats is currently floral. His idleness, he tells Reynolds, has alerted him to the "beauty of the morning" in a way that deliberate seeking never could. But before he gets too comfortable with his theory of indolence, he calls into question everything he has said—challenges his now too-busy ego. His sequence on idleness and spiders and bees "is a mere sophistication," a justification to "excuse [his] own indolence," even if his remarks "may neighbor" certain truths. Really, though, the correctness of his claims is beside the point; what matters is whether or not this letter has "lifted a little time" from his friend Reynolds's "shoulders."

This reversal, meant half seriously, mocks as pompous Keats's metaphor on the bee and the flower. The turnabout moreover emphasizes the true reason for the metaphor's existence in the first place—to cheer up a friend.

◆

Keats's quick questioning of his own conclusions forecasts a current in his odes: irony. Already present in earlier letters in which Keats undercuts his theories, this irony is Romantic—as opposed to dramatic, verbal, Socratic, and so on. Developed in the *Athenaeum Fragments* of the Schlegel brothers, this irony assumes that the universe is too abundant in energy and meaning to be represented by one system—philosophical, theological, political, scientific, artistic, poetic. To be romantically ironic, one must be aware of this gap between description and world, and express this awareness in word or image—create linguistic or visual works that present a multiplicity of views in conversation with one another, without any one position taking precedence over the others. The linguistic or pictorial plurality mimics the radical heterogeneity beyond, hints at its indescribable qualities. The more intricate the work, the closer it edges cosmic complexity. The grander the failure, the nearer success.[4]

In *Don Juan*, Byron creates a self-conscious narrator who comments on what he writes as he is composing, highlighting the fact that he could have chosen to write otherwise, that this text is but one fabrication among infinite concoctions. Coleridge's irony relies on the fragment, and appears in "Kubla Khan," subtitled "A Fragment," and *Christabel*, published in an incomplete form. These fragments, like all particles, inspire readers to imagine the unrealized whole, an effort requiring endless work, for completeness is forever inaccessible. Extreme finitude hints at bewildering infinity.

Keats in his letters unsays what he asserts, but doesn't invalidate the former claim. Hunt is biased yet objective. Wordsworth is an egotist but sublime. Keats's ideas on the power of passiveness are valid and silly. The knowing a-logic of the words conjures the unknowable logic of the world.

In a late-February letter to Taylor, Keats proclaims an ironic poetics, emphasizing meanings too immense for verse. His first axiom: "poetry should surprise by a fine excess and not by Singularity." Poetry should transcend the poet's perspective, point to a multitude of incongruous visions, ranging from Cordelia to Macbeth. Poetry like this can "strike" readers of many different viewpoints, expressing their "own highest thoughts" so fittingly as to "appear—almost a remembrance." A second axiom also recommends excess. The "touches of Beauty should never be half way therby making the reader breathless instead of content: the rise, the progress, the setting of imagery should like the Sun come natural to him—shine over him and set soberly although in magnificence leaving him in the Luxury of twilight." Experiencing words as he would the twilight, lambently somber, is not terribly difficult for an impassioned reader. But creating such complex verse is a fact that leads Keats to a third axiom: if poetry doesn't come "as naturally as the leaves to the tree," it shouldn't come at all.

✦

Keats consolidates these new discoveries of the winter of 1818 in one of the only notable poems from this time, "When I Have Fears That I May Cease to Be," a sonnet from January 31. The poem opens in fear—that he, the poet, might die before he has "gleaned [his] teeming brain" and created books that will hold his ripe harvest like "rich garners." In particular, he is afraid that he'll fail to translate into verse, with "the magic hand of chance," the sky's "huge cloudy symbols of a high romance." He is moreover anxious over the brief span of time he has left to cultivate actual romance. Before long, he won't be able to look upon his beloved, "fair creature of an hour," and so will be bereft of the "faery power of unreflecting love."

"You don't have much time to write and love." This is the message of the first twelve lines. We expect a final turn to carpe diem: "Better write and love now, hard; burn out, don't fade away." But Keats destroys this expectation, dramatically. He breaks into line twelve with a dash:

> Never have relish in the faery power
> Of unreflecting love;—then on the shore
> Of the wide world I stand alone, and think
> Till love and fame to nothingness do sink.

This is more memento mori than carpe diem. The poet realizes that poetic fame is tenuously based on "cloudy symbols," "shadows," "magic," and "chance"; and that his amorous longing is "unreflecting," longing for an ephemeral, undefined "creature." And these superficial yearnings don't just stupefy him with fantasy; they enclose him in a diminutive mist, hindering meaningful, expansive contact with the "wide world." Once these illusions fade, the poet stands alone before the actual, on a boundary between earth and sea, and reflects. He has in an instant transformed: from Endymion-like seeker after ideal beauty to Shakespearean quester for raw experience, from narcissistic dreamer ("I want the world to fit my fantasies") to disinterested thinker ("let things be").

What this poet first beholds after he awakens is: nothing. Fame and love dissolve into this state. But the nothingness is also the world beyond our words and concepts: no-*thing* to our mind's maps. This void is a plentitude, everything at once, all existence before we name it or conceive it. To apprehend this fullness, we must achieve negative capability, not commit overly to one position or another—to *something*—and be ready for whatever arises. Irony is required for this loose stance, holding lightly to beliefs or interpretations, taking them seriously when they enrich life, mocking them, genially, if they don't.

Chapter 7

Mist

Keats didn't content himself long with his January and February conclusions. Though he didn't renounce them—they are parts of his most mature poetical and ethical visions—he altered them quickly. A primary reason for his change was the grueling work he did during the spring of 1818: all alone, he cared for the consumptive Tom. Ministering to his brother's heavy needs, Keats found it impossible to cultivate egolessness. He had to muster will, assert an "I."

Keats's new role as his brother's nurse began when George appeared in London in late February or early March. George and Tom had been spending the winter in Teignmouth, a small ocean-side village in Devonshire, hoping that the sea air would help Tom's lungs. Keats had told his brothers in December that he would soon join them there. But he balked. Life in Hampstead was too stimulating, socially and intellectually. Then George unexpectedly showed. He had just turned twenty-one, and was eager to establish a career and get married. He required time in London to negotiate his inheritance with Abbey and come to an understanding with Georgiana Wylie, his sweetheart.

Tom was too sick to travel or remain alone. John took a coach to the seaside on March 4, freezing through one of the worst storms to hit England in years. The wetness proved portentous: it rained almost every day during Keats's two months in Teignmouth.

Devonshire—"splashy, rainy, misty, snowy, foggy, haily floody, muddy slipshod"—put Keats in a terrible mood. Nothing pleased about the place. The hills might be beautiful; the primroses and cliffs, too—but he could never see them for the "fog, hail, snow rain—Mist—blanketing" the coast "three parts of the year." The women are like "London people in a sort of negative way," and the men are "the poorest creatures in England." A month of this dreariness weighed him down "completely."

Environment aside, there was Tom. He suffered coughing fits, chest pains, bloody phlegm, breathing difficulty, headaches, vomiting, fever, chills, night sweats, loss of appetite, confusion, seizures. John was right there with him, night and day, buoying his spirits, keeping him cool or warm as needed, feeding him, cleaning his linen and clothes. When he had brief rests from these duties, he was too tired to read or write, and he had no friends with whom to converse. And he didn't want to go out into the chilling mist.

"Mist" appears repeatedly Keats's correspondence during this time, and it doesn't just stand for the foggy weather. It also serves as a metaphor for mental haziness. He calls the confusing Greek in a Milton poem a "mistiness," and likens adult bewilderment to stumbling into a "Mist."

Depressed, exhausted, Keats was sick of cognitive mists. He craved clarity: what "a happy thing it would be if we could settle our thoughts, make our minds up on any matter in five Minutes and remain content— that is to build a sort of mental Cottage of feelings quiet and pleasant—to have a sort of Philosophical Back Garden, and cheerful holiday-keeping front one—but Alas! this can never be."

To suspend the ego, to be no one in particular: these practices thrive when a man is fairly sure of who he is and what's going on, when he senses his power, potential. But when this same man is unsure of himself, when he's not certain who's there when he says his name, when everything he's accomplished so far seems shoddy and when the future appears as one long malaise, then this man must balance suspension with assertion, must project his feelings and thoughts onto the world, be somebody, *positively* capable.

Only a week into Devon's mist, Keats realizes this. In his first letter to Bailey from the coast, he startlingly questions his cherished vocation: "I am sometimes so very skeptical as to think Poetry itself a mere Jack a lanthern to amuse whoever may chance to be struck with its brilliance." With this thought in mind, the negatively capable poet proposes a radical notion: "probably every mental pursuit takes its reality and worth from the ardour of the pursuer." Poetry and indeed everything else are not intrinsically valuable or even durable existences but rather projections of the mind, imaginings. The world is not found but made. There is no extramental reality over which to be uncertain.

Keats amplifies. "[B]eing in itself," might be "a nothing"; however, three kinds of "Ethereal thing[s]"—things made by the mind—"may at least be . . . real." The first of these airy elements are "Things real," "such as existences of Sun Moon & Star and passages of Shakespeare." This is the object world, the palpable stuff that we actively imbue with meaning, making it real in relation to our needs and desires. We transform scattered stars into significant constellations, or words on a page to this interpretation or that.

Next are "Things semireal such as Love, and Clouds &c which require a greeting of the Spirit to make them wholly exist." These are wispier occurrences, events lacking solidity. To clarify these currents, slow them to concept and value, requires more active projection: dividing barely visible or unseen turbulence into vectors, directions, polarities. Cognition in this case recalls the deity brooding over chaos, speaking it into light and dark.

The last of the "Ethereal thing[s]" are the "Nothings which are made Great and dignified by an ardent pursuit—Which by the by stamps the burgundy mark on the bottles of our Minds, insomuch as they are able to *consec[r]ate whate'er they look upon.*'" If the first category describes solid matter, and if the second betokens slippery happenings, physical or mental, then this third division signifies acts purely of the mind, births of the brain that vitalize their origin. The mind, like fermenting wine, generates ecstatic visions; if ardently pursued—that is, intensely imagined—these visions become as palpable as actual beings, with power to stamp the label of the bottle from which they sprang. The mind fashions a poem; the poem inspires the mind; the mind, expanded, creates deeper, richer art, which elevates and widens the mind even more, and so on.

This process reverberates back to Keats's second category of insubstantial "things": the "semi-real." "The greeting of the spirit" by which the mind vivifies evanescent feelings and phantom currents also implies a fruitful interchange between the mind and the event on which it focuses. To greet someone is a deliberate choice to hail, hospitably, his presence. While giving out cheer, the greeter receives good will himself, the return of respect. His charity goes out and comes back. The same structure underlies the creation of "things real." The mind is stimulated more by some objects—suns, moons, Shakespeare sonnets—than others, and transforms these objects into livelier, more meaningful creatures.

Keats finds a middle way between the egolessness he was extolling weeks earlier and the pride he was admonishing in his friends. Generosity toward the world; passivity before the "stamp" of externals, whether imagined or palpable: these characteristics recall negative capability. But "ardor" here is the ground of all perception, the urge to make the world meaningful through varying degrees of mental activity.

M. H. Abrams's famous metaphor of the mind as mirror and lamp is pertinent: mind reflecting, mind imbuing. But Keats provides his own figure for the mind that shapes what it finds. After copying a sonnet on analogies between the seasons and the mind, he details one of his "old maxim[s]": "every point of thought is the centre of an intellectual world—the two uppermost thoughts in a Man's mind are the two poles of his World he revolves on them and every thing is southward or northward to him through their means." Each of us dwells within an intellectual world of our own fashioning, a sphere revolving around the poles of our most cherished thoughts. The surface of this planet is porous, receiving currents from the atmosphere and organizing them into quadrants—north, south, east, and west. According to the organizing principle, potentially different for each mind-world, a thing can appear as "feathers" or "iron." This process of imbibing and transmuting is not static—each new thought becomes a new center of the sphere, and so rearranges the poles, and shifts the vectors through which experience flows. An active mind is an ever-evolving planet interacting with its atmosphere in perpetually novel ways.

Keats mocks these ponderous musings. He confesses to Bailey that he has not "one Idea of the truth of any of my speculations." "I shall never be a Reasoner because I care not to be in the right, when retired from bickering and in a proper philosophical temper." Given this flippant attitude, he might in the future "endeavour to prove that Apollo as he had cat gut strings to his Lyre used a cats' paw as a Pecten—and further from said Pecten's reiterated and continual teasing came the term Hen peck'd."

✦

A week deeper into his dreary 1818 sojourn in Teignmouth, the mental and physical mist thickening, Keats tried to cheer himself once more with humor, but the jokes quickly choked, as he began to wonder if arduous projection of self onto world, no matter how sensitive to nuances and complexities, might lead to solipsism and consequent despair.

It is March 25. Keats tries to write a funny verse letter to Reynolds. He describes the night before, when, as he lay in bed, "Shapes, and Shadows and Remembrances" flew willy-nilly before his eyes: "[t]wo witch's eyes above a cherub's mouth, / Voltaire with casque and shield and habergeon, / And Alexander with his night-cap on." He saw Socrates "a tying his cravat," too, and Hazlitt "playing with Miss Edgworth's cat," and a famous actor, Junius Brutus, drunk. A lucky few in their dreams avoid this surreal bizarreness, he adds, and envision beauty. This minority, poets, enjoy in the darkness flowers, harps, artful color, exotic scenes, enchanted lands.

Keats laments that all of our "dreamings" don't take their "colours from the sunset." Unfortunately, most of our reveries "shadow" how "our soul's day-time" turmoil agitates the "dark void of night." This quotidian jostling demoralizes Keats, cleaving a rift between what he desires and what is: "Things cannot to the will / Be settled, but they tease us out of thought." (Keats will use this last clause in his "Ode on a Grecian Urn," to express similar befuddlement.)

But the world's intractability isn't the cause of our unhappiness. The origin lies in our own imaginations. Not constrained by "any standard law / Of either heaven or earth," imagination can fly beyond "its proper bound." However, it never sheds the individual fears and desires from which it ascended, and so hovers awkwardly between the ignorance that projected it and the sublime to which it aspires. Floating in "a sort of purgatory blind," imagination seduces us to envision something different from what we currently possess, but it can't deliver the object. Unsatisfied with summer's joys, we yearn for the opposite: seriousness, grieving. We don't enjoy the nightingale's song; some hymn more beautiful exists, compared to which, this bird is off tune.

Keats knows this dejection. Earlier, he sat reading on a "lampit rock of green seaweed / Among the breakers." The evening was quiet; the sea, tranquil. He felt "at home / And should have been most happy." But his imagination strained to glimpse beyond his place. He gazed "too far out into the sea; where every maw / The greater on the less feeds evermore." Into these engulfing waters he imaginatively peers, and there sees "into the core / Of an eternal fierce destruction." Not content with contentment, he pictures, seemingly against his will, the opposite, and his happiness drains. Even now he is heartsick. His gathering of leaves, periwinkles, and wild strawberries has not helped. In his mind remain massacres. He imagines the shark savaging fish; a hawk pouncing; the robin "ravening a worm."

The mind's power to create things real, things semi-real, and no-things is dangerous. Sure, a poet can imbue the earth with gleams not there in the matter, with significance, too, as well as dignity and worth—the transformation of time's monotonous clicking into singsong rhythms. But this is a poet generously disposed, glad to greet the world. What of one more petulant? His imagination is still robust, but now in service of a malcontent master bent not on hailing the present moment, but rejecting it for something different, perhaps worse, maybe better—but definitely different. This action is excessive, superfluous, perverse: the turning of an event, for no apparent reason, into its contrary.

An extremely potent imagination is required for these conversions. It must be capacious, negatively capable in fact, able to picture two opposing views at once, both summer skies and frozen grounds. And it also necessitates empathy, the capacity to live into each conflicting perspective, to embody June and January. Finally, this kind of imagination depends upon irony, the power to affirm and deny simultaneously: summer is exquisite yet oppressive; winter freezes but reconciles one to the real.

Keats possesses such an imagination, but he doesn't yet know what it's capable of. He is a young pilot flying a state-of-the-art jet, and he wants to see what it can do. Can it perform glorious loops and dives, to the delight of those below? Can it help these groundlings by rapidly transporting food to those in need? Yes, but what else? What are its weapons?

Knowledge does not temper power. This is psychologically perilous. Keats becomes sea as well as selfless, anything, or nothing. He loses solidity, though, becomes fully his fears or desires, a sad inhabitant of his own anxious head.

How to avoid this solipsism? Keats wasn't aware of this question earlier, in Hampstead, when he imagined himself as a personless conduit through which externals would unobstructed flow. But finding himself engulfed in Devonshire mist and aggressively asserting a self: now he apprehends the perils of his grotesquely potent brain. He knows that he might turn Hamlet, muddying earth to his mind's dull Denmark.

This isn't to say that Keats before nursing Tom was entirely unaware of the dangers of introspection. In "On First Looking into Chapman's Homer" and "On Seeing the Elgin Marbles," he described how overemphasizing the mind's images can sever one from physical vitality. In each of those poems, however, mental industriousness is but a preparation for sublime vision. The mind's seductions, tepid and nebulous, don't threaten. Now, however, a year later, violent, blinding, they do, and Keats knows it. And with his more acute consciousness of how sinister self-absorption can be, arises a sharper understanding of how necessary, for thriving, experience of the outer world is.

Keats's preternatural ability to self-correct saved him from solipsism. This time, he didn't wait for the sensual world to come to him, with its Isle of Wight jackdaws and Hampstead meadow grass. He went to it, deliberately, forcefully. A mere two weeks after his ominous letter to Reynolds on the mind's menace, Keats wrote to Haydon of his purpose to take, "within a Month," "a pedestrian tour through the North of England, and part of Scotland." He would do so as a "Prologue to the Life" he intends to pursue, one of writing, studying, and traveling. The most important reason for his trip, though, is to gain traction in earth's altitudes. He will "clamber through the Clouds and exist," get "such an accumulation of stupendous recollections that as I walk through the suburbs of London

I may not see them—I will stand upon Mont Blanc and remember this coming Summer when I intend to straddle ben Lomond."

Though Keats is still enamored of his mind's ability to blot out his environment—London with memories of the mountains—he now thirsts for knowledge, as he writes on April 24, that will do "some good for the world." A week later, he praises practical knowledge—of law, of medicine—for saving us from bias and connecting us to "a great whole." He is glad of his surgical skills, and might even study his medical books again. Such labor, as with all efforts to master a field, "takes away the heat and fever; and helps, by widening speculation, to ease the Burden of the Mystery," a Wordsworth phrase signifying the weight of the tragic world. Practical knowing discloses nature's lilting.

To develop this idea, Keats recovers a metaphor from his verse epistle to Reynolds. In that piece, remember, Keats depicted imagination divorced from the world as a poor blind creature hovering between the earth it disdains and the heavens for which it hungers. Here, he claims that when we experience "high Sensations" but lack the knowledge to give them meaningful form, we are "falling continually ten thousand fathoms deep and being blown up again without wings and with all [the] horror of a bare shoulderd Creature." An untethered imagination, chaotic sensations: both lead to flawed flight—respectively, to a mind stuck in air, or one flitting wildly about. Knowledge tames these unruly aerials. It gives us wings, and "we go thro' the same air and space without fear."

But can this sort of knowledge solace us when those we love die or we ourselves are hurt and confused? Keats considers this more complicated matter in a famous simile. Imagine life as "a large Mansion of Many Apartments, two of which [he] can only describe, the doors of the rest being yet shut upon [him]." The first of these rooms open to him is the "the infant or thoughtless Chamber, in which we remain as long as we do not think." Young, unformed, uninformed, we remain in this comfortable chamber a long time, even though "the doors of the second Chamber remain wide open, showing a bright appearance." Eventually, we waken into thought—become self-aware, curious—and venture into this "Chamber of Maiden-Thought." There we rise to full awareness of our innocence. We enjoy the state and know we are enjoying it. The room intoxicates us with its "light" and "atmosphere." We ponder "delaying there for ever in delight." But as we mature, we learn, want to know more, and soon contemplate "the heart and nature of Man." Then, trouble: we realize that "the World is full of Misery and Heartbreak, Pain, Sickness and oppression." The darkness subsumes the room's light, and numerous doors open, "all leading to dark passages—We see not the balance of good and evil. We are in a Mist—*We* are now in that state—We feel the 'burden of the Mystery.' "

Wordsworth reached this point; his verse explores these gloomy corridors. Groping in a mist all spring, Keats has reached this juncture as well, stands suspended before the several thresholds, ready to step into a third room. He trusts that in this chamber he will discover knowledge of "something real in the World."

How can the mist, physical and mental pain, teach us what is real? When we suffer, we realize that what endures in life, what persistently shapes and drives us, is: we lose what we love. If we are brave enough to accept this, if we don't repress or deny it, then we prepare ourselves for the most important labor: trying to view the suffering positively, as an invitation to discover what we need to stay alive, not just maintain basal metabolic rate, but thrive, embrace the grit and grandeur both, Devon's cruel fogs and autumn's fruitfulness. And what we need to flourish, Keats already guesses and soon will tenaciously grasp, is imagination, our ability to absorb what is—never fully knowable, always bereaving us—and transform this "isness" into meaningful events: the passing year into the four seasons' dance, depression into salutary purging of illusion, terminal illness into last touches more intense than those of the first and middle times.

Keats exemplifies this sort of imagining in creating his simile. He is engulfed in the Devon haze, baffled, sad, anxious. He faces the fog, unafraid, but needs a lighthouse. He builds it himself, in his "life-as-mansion" trope, a luminous picture of artistic development, a Bildungsroman in miniature. The image of the house first of all gives time and space a cogent form—self-contained, organized, safe. The sequencing of rooms suggests a deeper order: life has a clear beginning—a front portal—and a well-defined end—a back egress. The physical figures the psychological: a poet develops from unconscious innocence, to innocence aware of itself, to intimations of experience, to experience proper, bleak but revelatory. Each stage, each room, exudes a particular feeling—pleasure, bliss, doubt—and a corresponding depth of knowledge, ranging from untroubled ignorance to portentous confusion.

Keats's conceit throbs between Dickinson's ecstatic image of the poet's life as "more numerous of Windows—/ Superior—for Doors" and F. Scott Fitzgerald's more frightening metaphor of mental breakdown: "a little boy left alone in a big house, who knew that now he could do anything he wanted to do, but found that there was nothing that he wanted to do."[1] But even though Keats's simile is realistically aware of life's inscrutable tragedies, it is patently a fiction: a fantasy of order over chaos,

progression over accident. How is it different from the dangerous reveries Keats describes in his verse epistle to Reynolds, those petulant mental
fabrications that imprison us in our own vexed skulls? In this way: Keats's
mansion doesn't *oppose* his troubled existential condition, merely shelter
him from the anguish; it accounts for the horror of being alive—it's like
stumbling into a strange room where no lamps are—as well as for the
equally valid feeling that there is meaning in the madness. Suicidal brooding can become imaginative compassion.

Art is hope at its most potent: despair opening to other hearts. The
more tragic the event, the more powerful the art. Think of the hurt that
produced *Hamlet*, or the agony behind Keats's nightingale ode.

Chapter 8

Sore Throat

In mid-May of 1818, Keats returned to London. He attended George's wedding to Georgiana and saw the couple off on their voyage to America. He also fell ill.

Late in the month, he wrote to Bailey, "I have this morning such a Lethargy that I cannot write. . . . I am now so depressed that I have not an Idea to put to paper—my hand feels like lead—and yet it is an unpleasant numbness it does not take away the pain of existence—I don't know what to write." He then wonders if his sorrow is more connected to body than mind: "my intellect must be in a degen[er]ating state—it must be for when I should [be] writing about god knows what I am troubling you with Moods of my own Mind or rather body—for Mind there is none. I am in that temper that if I were under Water I would scarcely kick to come to the top."

About two weeks later, Keats worries about his physical health again, in another letter to Bailey, admitting that he might not be able to travel north because "of [his] brother Tom and a little indisposition of [his] own." A few days earlier, on June 6, he betrays that he is quite sick. The "doctor says [he] mustn't go out."

Consumption's symptoms had begun their slow, sinister work. For the rest of his life, Keats battled against them—fatigue, fever, sore throat—and against the mental anguish of knowing that anything he started—a poem, a romance might not reach fruition.

Keats already had mortality on his mind in Devonshire. How could he not, nursing a dying brother and still traumatized by his mother's death from the same illness? In his letters, focused on matters aesthetic and epistemological, he hid his fears of his own body's ailments. But he couldn't conceal anatomical terror entirely. The death skull peered out from the oddest of places, the romance *Isabella,* which Keats composed, mostly in secret, during his hours away from the sickroom.

The plot, drawn from Boccaccio's *Decameron,* is simple. Isabella, a young woman from a Florentine merchant family, falls in love with a clerk, Lorenzo. Her two greedy brothers refuse the match. They want Isabella to marry money, and Lorenzo is poor. They murder him. To cover their crime, they tell Isabella that her lover has left the country on a business trip. Isabella pines, until one night, Lorenzo appears to her in a dream, and tells her of her siblings' crime. She digs him up, cuts off his head, hides it under the soil in a basil pot. She sits by the herb and mourns. Her brothers steal the pot, find the head, flee Florence. Once Isabella finds that her pot has disappeared, she dies of sorrow.

The poem overall is not one of Keats's best. However, two passages stand out as some of the most ferociously gruesome writing in the nineteenth century. In the first, Keats describes the horrors perpetrated by the brothers' global capitalism. In service of their rapacious business, many a "weary hand did swelt / In torched mines and noisy factories." Many others, whose loins were once "proud-quiver'd," did "melt / In blood from stinging whip." Yet others stood in a river "with hollow eyes," mining the "rich-ored drifting of the flood." Worse still was the siblings' treatment of "the Ceylon diver." For these greedy merchants, the diver "held his breath / And went all naked to the hungry shark"; his "ears gush'd blood." Other creatures suffered even more horrifically. A "seal on the cold ice with piteous bark / Lay full of darts." A thousand men "seethe[d]" in "troubles wide and dark," ignorantly turning a wheel "that set sharp racks at work, to pinch and peel."

Keats description of Lorenzo's ghost is equally lurid. In Isabella's dream, the dead lover stands with his "glossy hair," which once "could shoot / Lustre into the sun," "marr'd." The "forest tomb" has done this matting, as it has also "put cold doom / Upon his lips, and taken the soft lute / From his lorn voice." His grave has also "past his loamed ears" made a "miry channel for his tears." When this "pale shadow" speaks, he stammers, heaves, stutters, grunts, his tongue now "piteous."

Bodies writhing, burned, pierced, bleeding from orifices; bodies on the verge of hollow-eyed dying, or dead; pain's rictus; black lips, a putrid cheek. These are a medical student's rendering of the symptoms of tuberculosis. Beside these physiological horrors—real body-rot, green-brown, reeking, making you puke—Gothic conventions, with their rattling chains and night moans, are silly.

Keats's soul-vision is an effort to find meaning in these most demeaning portions of life. As he journeys north, trying to enjoy nature's scenes despite his ailments, he begins to realize that illness, properly seen, is not opposed to beauty but actually an integral part of it. The sickbed lies on Helicon.

◆

In June 1818, Keats, with Brown as a traveling companion, headed north-ward, to the third room, trusting that the journey would give him "more experience, rub off more Prejudice, use [him] to more hardship, identify finer scenes, load [him] with grander Mountains, and strengthen more [his] reach in Poetry than would stopping at home among [his] books."

Wishing to cheer his sick brother who could not travel—and also per-haps compensating for his guilt over not staying with him—Keats wrote Tom detailed letters about his trip. This extemporaneous travelogue is a fas-cinating conflict between hardship and grandeur, in which sublime scenes and sore throats enter into a mutually causal relationship: the hurt body intensifies grace, which in turn reveals the full significance of the strain.

Fittingly, his first letter from the road, dated June 25 and posted from Lancaster, shows him rising one morning at four and stepping into a "Scotch mist." His and Brown's first stop was Windermere, in the south-ern portion of the Lake District, only seven miles from Ambleside, where Wordsworth was currently living. When Keats at dinner asked a waiter about Wordsworth, the man said that he knew the poet, that Wordsworth had been in the establishment only a few days earlier canvassing, much to the liberal Keats's dissatisfaction, for a Tory candidate for Parliament. Keats wasn't disappointed for long, though. The scenery heartened him, as it had Wordsworth. He writes to Tom that his views of the water "can never fade away—they make one forget the divisions of life; age, youth, poverty and riches; and refine one's sensual vision into a sort of north star which can never cease to be open lidded and stedfast over the wonders of the great Power."

The next day, gazing on mountains and waterfalls, he is similarly changed, once more claiming that certain sensual experiences endure, even outlasting the creations of the imagination and the archives of memory. "What astonishes me more than anything," he proclaims, "is the tone, the coloring, the slate, the stone, the moss, the rock-weed; or, if I may so say, the intellect, the countenance of such places. The space, the magnitude of mountains and waterfalls are well imagined before one sees them; but this countenance or intellectual tone must surpass every imagi-nation and defy any remembrance." This rugged ambience has something to teach him: "I shall learn poetry here and shall henceforth write more than ever, for the abstract endeavor of being able to add a mite to that mass of beauty which is harvested from these grand materials, by the fin-est spirits, and put into ethereal existence for the relish of one's fellows. I cannot think with Hazlitt that these scenes make man appear little. I never forget my stature completely—I live in the eye; my imagination, surpassed, is at rest."

In both passages, Keats expresses a paradox that will continue to occupy him: the most ephemeral experiences, those of the senses, can become, if sufficiently intense, the most permanent. The initial passage—which points ahead to the sonnet "Bright Star"—asserts that vigorous sensual encounters are eternal. The eternity, however, even if likened to the North Star, is not static, cold. It resembles more the unchangeableness that Keats will describe in the sonnet, in contrast to the star—the warm dynamic permanence of living-dying rhythms, such as a "fair love's ripening breast," with its "soft fall and swell," or Lake Windermere's shimmering undulations, ripples of an abiding, animating force. This durability is organic, not supernatural: it depends on the vitality of the transience, the velocity with which a physical event strikes the senses. The more momentum at impact, the more deeply stamped onto the fibers, the more likely to persist, to become the "moments of being" Virginia Woolf worships.

However laboriously we try to picture future "moments of being" or compare them to the past, the actual experience—unprecedented, unrepeatable, unpredictable—eludes imagination and memory. Escaping these faculties is the "intellect" or the "countenance" of the galvanizing scenes. The tone, the coloring, the texture of the rocks, the moss, the weeds: these cohere before the poet's refined senses into a unified expression, a mood, a face. This cogent visage, the wild taking on significant human form, is what astonishes Keats most about his Lake District visions. His acute senses, usually conduits of raw data, can forge import just as effectively as memory and imagination can generate denotation and connotation, information and nuance. He counters Hazlitt, who believes that nature's grandeur minimizes human stature. Keats holds that the senses, if subtle enough, can discern grand enduring rhythmic forms that in turn can inspire a poet to create his own gorgeous, kinetic patterns, "ethereal" existences his readers can relish.

Keats's journey into the mist has so far, during the first two days, done exactly what he wanted it to. He has widened his experiences, questioned assumptions, stretched his poetic reach. He is feeling good, in body and mind. "I am well," he writes to Tom.

This bloom withers quickly. A few days later, after describing his and Brown's recent movements—from Ambleside to Mount Helvellyn to Keswick to the mountains of Borrowdale—he describes their ascent of Mount Skiddaw, England's highest peak. He began the climb already worn out from his ramblings around Borrowdale, and struggled to make the peak. Before reaching it, and the long view he desired, a "mist" (yet again) came upon him, and "shut out the view." Luckily, he was still able to command an extensive vista, since he was high enough "without mist" to where he could still see Scotland's coast, the Irish Sea, and many nearby peaks. But then he and Brown got the chills, needing rum for warmth and gumption. On the final ascent, the air soaked them through, like a "cold bath."

From this moment in his trip onward, Keats slaved to shake the cold. On July 1, he and Brown crossed the Scottish border into Carlisle and then pushed on to Dumfries, where they visited the tomb of Robert Burns. There Keats wrote a sonnet. The darkness of the verse is striking—a grisly cold up-gush of the depression Keats was trying to suppress. The village, the clouds, the trees, and the hills surrounding the tomb are, though beautiful, "cold—strange—as in a dream" from long ago, now "new begun." This icy dream, sent from the chills of "winter's ague," overwhelms the "short-lived, paly summer," shrinking it to "one hour's gleam," which, even though "sapphire warm," beams no stars. The stark conclusion: "All is cold Beauty; pain is never done." The "real of beauty," freed from "dead hue / Fickly [fickle] imagination and sick pride," is "wan." Only after these repeated associations of beauty with coldness, illness, and death, does Keats turn to the subject of the sonnet: "Burns! with honor due / I have oft honoured thee. Great shadow; hide / Thy face—I sin against native skies."

This is bizarre. Why would a Keats who has spoken with authority for the first twelve lines, making strong claims on the nature of beauty and life, suddenly say that in honoring Burns, he sins, and that the shadow of Burns shouldn't even look at him? Keats's thinking might have gone like this. "The beauty to which I have aspired is not vital but cold and moribund, and so is Tom and so I might be soon myself; pain is all there is, and it doesn't stop. But this is nonetheless the reality I want to explore—seeking the third room. If this is indeed the actual—beauty is death, life is pain—then where is value? What's the point of writing poetry, of attempting to be a great poet? Everything is worthless. I am worthless. For me even to think I can honor another poet is hubris."

The poem betrays Keats's anxieties at this early juncture of the trip. He is worried over sickness—of body and of spirit. He is cold, again, on psychological and physical levels. And this freezing and this fret are weakening his confidence as a poet.

The poem also expresses, however, Keats's attempt to connect suffering and beauty. Pain is chronic, illness, too, and dying, but this all-consuming coldness is beautiful. Keats doesn't say exactly how but he does offer a hint: beauty is icy because death is its origin. Creatures are finite, and become colder, closer to the sepulcher, with every breath; the poet reminds us of this passing, urges us to say to those most gorgeous flashes, sadly, ecstatically: freeze.

During the next weeks, Keats nears reality's frigid innards. From Dumfries, he and Brown travel to Wigan, on Scotland's southwestern coast, where Keats is disgusted by the oppressive Scottish "kirkmen." Then the two men sail to Ireland's northeast coast. They spend several days sightseeing on the Giant's Causeway, in Donaghadee and Belfast. Ireland's squalor appalls Keats, the "nakedness, the rags, the dirt and misery." The weather doesn't help. He trudges over peat bogs—"dreary, black, dank, flat and spongy"—in incessant cold rain.

Keats and Brown return from Ireland earlier than planned. The weather and walking have taken their toll on the poet. In a letter to Reynolds composed in mid-July, he compares Reynolds's happiness—the man recently got engaged—to his own dejection. His "sensations are sometimes deadened for weeks together," and this despair has often set him yearning for domestic comfort. The possibility of attaining this serenity has made him "resolve to have a care of [his] health." This resolution implies Keats is currently *not* caring for his well-being. He rallies, however. He reports that he and Brown are bearing "the fatigue very well," covering, on foot, about twenty miles a day.

The cheer, probably feigned, is brief. His mood worsens, and stays foul. For the rest of the summer, he complains about the weather, mainly the rain, which either confines him and Brown to their quarters or soaks their hearts through. He bemoans the food as well, coarse, dirty, consisting mostly of eggs. Squalid accommodations bring him down, too. After a long day of hiking through Mull's mucky bogs—sometimes barefooted, to keep shoes and socks somewhat dry—he and Brown bed down in a "Shepherd's Hut, into w[h]ich [they] could scarcely get for the smoke through a door lower than [his] shoulders." The rafters and turf-thatched roof are smoke-blackened; the floor, earth, "full of hills and dales." The travelers sleep in their wet clothes.

From this hellish night in Mull, July 22, onward, Keats is rarely without a sore throat. He first mentions it to Tom, admitting that it is severe enough to lay him up a few days in Oban. Over a week later, in another letter to his brother, he notes that his "sore throat is not quite well." He intends on "stopping," once again, for a few days. Then, in his next letter, the last of his trip, addressed to Georgiana's mother and dated August 6, he confesses the extent of his misery. "I have got wet through day after day, eaten oak cake, & drank whiskey, walked up to my knees in Bog, got a sore throat."

The damp, suffocating night in Mull revealed to him the fate he had most feared, intimated in a letter he wrote to Bailey from the island: "I trust we shall see you ere long in Cumberland—at least I hope I shall before my visit to America more than once I intend to pass a while year with George if I live to the completion of my three next."

Set the spookiness of the final clause aside—Keats would die two years and seven months later—and grasp the gravity: John Keats is *certain* he is going to die soon.

✦

In the early spring of 2012, I led a group of undergraduates to the Lake District. We hoped to deepen our understanding of Wordsworth. The Lake Poet and his daffodils, though, were just then tepid to me, for Keats and death were pressing my mind.

Only a week earlier, I had followed my visit to Keats's house in Hampstead with a trip to the Old Operating Theatre Museum in Southwark. In this museum remains the auditorium in which the medical student Keats watched his professors dissect cadavers, amputate living limbs, remove kidney stones. The horrors of these spectacles I have reported, but I have not yet said what meaning the theater held for me.

I have never much liked history as a subject, probably because I have trouble reimagining the past. Call it a lack of empathy, that cardinal Keats virtue; or, more generously, term it an engrossment in the now. But that day in the operating theater was different, for one reason: teeth marks.

The actual lecture space, made to look as it would have in Keats's day, bored me. I had perhaps already read too much about it or seen too many pictures. The various medical instruments of yore didn't interest me much either, beyond creepily recalling those weird instruments of gynecological torture in the Jeremy Irons film *Dead Ringers*. Then I happened upon the surgeon's stick, a cane about four feet long wrapped in leather strips. This was the instrument the surgeon's assistant forced into the mouths of the agonized patients, stifling their screams and buffering their grinding molars. I could still see the teeth imprints. I remembered the only time the dentist drilled me without deadening the nerves, and my jaws clamped and I shut my eyes.

I also thought, though (immediately distancing myself, out of fear, from the visceral): this object could be the subject of a good poem about a young Keats riveted upon the surgeon's butchery. I spent the next week trying to work it up. It never came off.

But the composing kept death and Keats close, so much so that what most excited me during my first hike in Wordsworth country (taking place, again, exactly a week after my visit to the operating theater) was not the sublime scenery but a sheep skull a few feet off the trail. Somewhat facetiously, I took this as an instance of Jungian synchronicity: my psyche mirrored in matter. I also thought: won't my students think this is cool? I secured the head on the back of my pack and descended to Dove Cottage, where I was scheduled to meet the group.

When my students saw the skull, they said nothing. They looked down awkwardly, and then walked into the house. Embarrassed, I removed the skull from my back, hid it in some tall grass. I would pick it up later.

Those bones spoiled my weekend. Now self-conscious around my students, I botched my remarks on the gorgeous landscape. I was also so enamored, secretly, of my skull, that I wanted another one. I kept my eyes on the ground, and missed the lacustrine vistas. I moreover brooded over Keats, ignored Wordsworth.

But I was actually neglecting Keats, too. Even though I replayed his Lake District and Scotland letters in my mind and connected these thoughts to the death imagery in the odes, I didn't *see* the poet but rather the long-standing idea through which I then viewed his work: the memento mori theme, "you must remember death if you want to embrace life."

(Or, "live every day as if it were your last," our modern version of the sentiment, as though one's last hours will be ecstatically beautiful, with each petal and breeze and touch becoming cosmically precious. The reality, though, is probably this: one's final breaths are an unendurable sentence of regret and terror and anticipation of relief.)

Now, two years after my visit to the Lakes, I am different. Una, my delight, each day pulls, because of her maturing, away, forging connections outside my sphere, needing, wanting me less and less. Her inevitable going has made me more alert to other painful finitudes. My older friends, in their early sixties, are getting sick and staying sick, can't kick addictions, talk about retiring. Both of my parents are ill, in their mid-seventies. Approaching fifty, I am finally, belatedly, growing up, realizing that what I earlier thought—"love is life"—is wrong, and that the truth is: "the more we love, the more we lose."

Initiated into hurts the ideas can't touch, I now believe that Keats, after that nightmarish night in Mull, would scoff at the old memento mori notion, and say, "*forget* death if you want to enjoy life." But he couldn't forget: every time he swallowed, the reaper scratched his throat. Realizing that he would never *not* be thinking of death, he would revise: "hate it, rage against it, thunder to it: 'No!'"

Keats saves me from clichés, conventions, childish collections of bones, Gothic posturing, reminding me, life is not theory but danger. Gasping in graveyard gases, he gets the real use of death: it is an enemy not to be befriended but defeated, cowed by mighty creations of consummate art. Don't place a skull on your desk. Display a Shakespeare bust.

But to overcome the foe, you've got to know him well, intimately, better than he knows himself: study the color of the lung hemorrhage to learn the cure for the disease. This is the paradox of Keats's close-to-the-bone sense of death: don't flee it but face it, make it your dark familiar, your inmost double, twin, lover, the necessary sinister silence your bright muse sings over.

I wish I had understood Keats this concretely as I slogged through the mists north of Windermere. I would have forsaken the skull and studied the scree, blocked out Keats and welcomed Wordsworth, the man of that hour. I would have more soberly taught my students about how the nature poet's "ever-more-about-to-be" always out-hopes the despairing "no-more-ever-again." I would have tried to do for them what Keats has done for me: redeem them from mere idea, reconcile them to rocks.

Chapter 9

✦

Leap of the Eye

Imagine the gumption it took for Keats to bear up under his death sentence, the effort required to pursue long-range projects—poems, friendships, romances—when he knew he probably wouldn't see them through. How did he elude full-bore despair? How did he in fact embrace, generously and with zeal, the world that was harrying him into the ground?

He celebrated his murderer myriad ways. His primary method: humbly submitting to fate—early death—while aggressively positing freedom—making art. This double vision, essential for soul-making, emerges in the same letter in which he envisions his own death three years hence. This is the place, remarkably, in which he announces why he wanted to go on his northward trip in the first place—expand his scope, sand down prejudice, expose himself to "hardship," amplify his poetry. In making this proclamation only a few sentences before he hints at his impending demise, he expresses his most complex, capacious, and potent vision yet.

Negative capability enables a poet to describe his subjects with vivid intimacy. Too much attunement to the outside, though, can exacerbate depression, when identity is in crisis. Dejected, one needs to strengthen the self, project it, shape experience to fit desire. But such mental activity, overdone, can be dangerous. It can entrap a person in his own sullen brain.

In his "life as a mansion" epistle, Keats finds a mean between suspension and projection: accept the horror, turn it to revelation. Standing on the median, he connects suffering and beauty: the more intense the suffering, the more powerful the art.

Keats's journey originated from his desire to forge this middle path. But what he encountered in the cold mists was a reality much more disturbing than the "hardship" he imagined: his body is decaying and dying fast, and so slowing his ability, if not paralyzing it, to move, muse, compose. You can't rest in uncertainty or reconnoiter the gloom or forge poems when you can barely swallow or stand. This is a circumstance impossible to embrace. To it, Keats says, "no." But at the same time: "yes," since this condition births Pacifics, Elgins, nightingales, "glob'd peonies."

In his death-omened letter to Bailey, Keats complains about his travels. His quest for the sublime has degraded to weary "mountaineer[ing]": "I have been among wilds and Mountains too much to break out much about the[i]r Grandeur. I have fed upon Oak cake—not long enough to be very attached to it—The first Mountains I saw [near Ambleside], though not so large as some I have since seen, weighed very solemnly upon me. The whole effect is wearing away—yet I like them mainely." The nadir of his darkened journey is Mull, a "horrid place," his mortality's apocalypse.

But even as a dejected Keats negates his northing, he affirms it. Although the conditions in Mull are hell, he must admit that he is "more comfortable than [he] could have imagined in such a place." The people on the island, too, are "very kind." For instance: "We lost our way yesterday and enquiring at a Cottage, a youn[g] Woman without a word threw on her cloak and walked a Mile in a missling rain and splashy way to put us right again." This evocative, dreamily beautiful image—Keats and Brown speechlessly following, through a merciless Scottish storm, a strange, hooded woman who restores them, Beatrice-like, to the right path—shows that Keats even at his most depressed remains sensitive to, and interested in, the mysterious earth, where flexibility and openness can always foster great radiant grace, brightest in the mist's gloom.

✦

Love what you hate, loathe what you love: to encompass this wrenching paradox requires a poetry supple and capacious enough to say "no," "yes," and "maybe" all at once.

An essential element of this complex poetics is alertness to the relief, ecstatic, when death's vise briefly relaxes. We've all had intimations: the dentist stops his drill, or the ibuprofen floods the torn knee. These are temporary fixes. What if you because of chronic pain were always on the verge of such liberations? That would be terrible, nothing you would ever want. But it could be sublime: perpetual expectation of ravishing release.

Keats presses on this edge on Staffa, before uncanny Fingal's Cave. His stop in awful Mull was in route to this uninhabited island in the Hebrides, made of immense basalt columns, hexagonal in shape, into which the waves over the eons have carved a colossal cavern. Named after Fingal, a hero of Celtic myth, the cave is seventy feet high and 250 feet deep. The vast arched ceiling has inspired travelers to liken the space to a Gothic cathedral. Not Keats, at least initially. "Suppose now," he writes to Tom, "the Giants who rebelled against Jove had taken a whole Mass of black Columns and bound them together like bunches of matches—and then with immense Axes had made a cavern in the body of these Columns—of course the roof and floor must be composed of the broken ends of the Columns."

What would be the purpose of the binding and the blows? Wanton brutishness, such as one might see in over-strong bored boys crashing out windows in a vacant house? Or crude art-making, composed of jagged half-symmetries and pre-geometrical fragments? Keats doesn't answer and quickly pulls back from this outlandish image to a more ordinary description.

The sea, he says, has actually hollowed out the cavern, and left an interior that does indeed resemble Gothic architecture. But this comparison doesn't hold: "for solemnity and grandeur [the cave] far surpasses the finest Cathedrall." With columns colored "a sort of black with a lurking gloom of purple therein," and with waves at its core crashing into cannon-sounds heard twelve miles away, the cave is more bizarre than any building, too enchanting to seem natural. As Keats and Brown approached Staffa by boat, "there was such a fine swell of the sea that the pillars appeared rising immediately out of the crystal." This is fairy lore, a fantastical edifice magically ascending from bejeweled waves.

But this image, like those preceding it, fails to capture accurately the enormity. "It is impossible," Keats writes, to "describe" the cave. He tries again, nonetheless, in a feeble poem about how the spirit of the place is Milton's Lycidas.

But real ecstasy has preceded this linguistic fatigue. Keats, as sick eagle, beholds phenomena-possessing powers he lacks: durability (stone ascendant for millennia, water explosively unceasing); expansiveness (gigantic caverns engulfing a sea that seems bottomless); beauty (purple-black pillars of basalt, honeycombed, with a heart-space through which surge aqua-turquoise waves). Activating his own remaining potencies, words and imagination, Keats gamely attempts to close the rift between his "sick and dying animal" and these "artifices of eternity." His efforts fail. The cave as bizarre, Lovecraft-like product of frustrated half-gods; as an unearthly cathedral, more solemn and grand than any man-made edifice; as miraculously rising fairy form: though provocative, none of these figures adequately limns the scene.

Faltering, these images succeed. That they even exist is victory: an ailing poet, though he knows he can't detail the exuberance he beholds, still musters brilliant analogies. Moreover, the very inability of the words to represent the cave actually enables them to illuminate the cave. The images strain logic: the Titan-bashed matchsticks are both artistic creations and aftermath of destruction; the "cathedral-far-surpassed" is cathedral and not; the pillars rising from crystal constitute at once figurative natural description and literal supernatural detailing. In canceling itself, being one thing and its opposite, each image highlights its inadequacy for clearly describing the world, revealing that it is *not* the object it means to represent. Showing what the world is not, each ironically discloses what the world is: something beyond verbal representation—alogical, manifold, perpetually transforming. Aesthetically rich verbal patterns, beyond logic, intricate, semantically shifty, do this negative work more compellingly and conclusively than denotative structures. Erasing themselves more emphatically, they more intensely signify what eludes their scripts. Remember Ishmael's negative aesthetic: while no one image can ever represent the whale, some come closer than others.

In his next letter to Tom, his last of the trip, dated August 3, Keats narrates another galvanizing verbal failure, this time on Scotland's Ben Nevis, the highest mountain in the United Kingdom. Near the top, he, Brown, and their guide run into an engulfing mist, through which they must grope for the rest of their ascent. Close to the pinnacle, the climbers come upon a "chasm of some hundred feet deep." While terrifying, these abysses, Keats proclaims, "are the finest wonder of the whole—the[y] appear great rents in the very heart of the mountain though they are not, being at the side of it, but other huge crags arising round it give the appearance . . . to Nevis of a shattered heart or Core in itself." To "give way" to these "tremendous" chasms, some of which drop 1,500 feet, is to "turn . . . giddy."

Keats's excitement increases when the mist fades and he can see the clouds play about the peaks: "there were large Clouds about attracted by old Ben to a certain distance so as to form as it appeared large dome curtains which kept sailing about, opening and shutting at intervals here and there and everywhere; so that although we did not see one vast wide extent of prospect all round we saw something perhaps finer—these cloud-veils opening with a dissolving motion and showing us the mountainous region beneath as through a loop hole."

By the time Keats reaches the top, the clouds are still shifting, now obstructing, now revealing, his prospects. When the sky does clear, he is, as on Staffa, stunned. "I do not know whether I can give you an Idea of the prospect from a large Mountain top. You are on a stony plain which of course makes you forget you are on any but low ground—the horizon or rather edges of this plain being about 4000 feet above the Sea hide all country immediately beneath you, so that the next objects you see all round next to the edges of the flat top are the Summits of Mountains of

some distance off." Moving about the summit, "you see more or less of
the near neighbor country according as the Mountain you stand upon is
in different parts steep or rounded—but the most new thing of all is the
sudden leap of the eye from the extremity of what appears a plain into so
vast a distance."

The mound on which Keats stands rises from a spreading mist, so thick
that it covers completely all that is below—smaller mountains, earth, sea.
Only surrounding peaks break the fog, rising themselves like mounds
from a whitish plain. As you meander around your own elevation, Keats
says, you can believe that the foggy surfaces are indeed expanses of flat
land, and begin to imagine these other peaks as nothing but little neighbor countries. But then, in an instant, reality rushes back, and your eye
springs, seeing now not level ground but vast vaporous gulfs dipping
precipitously between heaven-assaulting peaks miles from one another
distant.

The "sudden leap of the eye": this phrase concisely renders the kind
of perceiving Keats cultivates from now on. As his body slows, he sends
his eye on quick missions, to see all that is seemingly solid and static as
enlivening vagueness. This method is not arbitrary; nor is it fantastical. It
is a penetration of reality, which is irreducibly mysterious, a mist in which
one knows not the "balance of good and evil." Each mist is different,
though, and summons specific searches, unique maps.

Keats is ailing in Staffa, so fatigued it's hard to walk. He sends his eye
up into the colossal overarching basalt. The orb senses the stone's intractable weirdness, its inaccessibility to habitual thought and perception,
and starts to conjure images, word-coordinates particular to the place,
that get lost in mystery while illuminating it. He does the same amidst the
chasms of Nevis.

This leaping of the eye: the eye flying to what it is most likely to mis-
understand, or not understand at all. This counters the degenerative
failure of his body with the generative faltering of imagination. While
his anatomy loses potential, Keats intensifies the powers of his mind.
He perpetually casts it into inscrutabilities he can brood infinitely upon,
endlessly poeticize. Riddle is rapture, joy in the imagination's capacities
perpetually to explore, strive, doubt, affirm, create, destroy. What Keats
suspected in "On Seeing the Elgin Marbles" now becomes his deep bone's
gospel: falling short is rising to grace. Dickinson, Keats's brilliant American admirer, got, when not yet thirty, this marrow—"Water, Is taught by
thirst," and "Birds, by Snow"—and also the more sinister pith: "A Bomb
upon the Ceiling / Is an improving thing"; "it keeps the nerves progres-
sive / Conjecture flourishing."

Chapter 10

Women

Keats is no sage. The poor man was as tormented as the rest of us, and prone to fears, anxieties, narrowness, selfishness, stupidity. He was sometimes aware of these limits and tried to surpass them; he was at times blind to his faults.

With women, Keats was at his worst. (One wonders what he would have made of the belle of Amherst.) In the letter he sent to Bailey from Mull—the letter in which he articulates his potent coupling of death and joy—he admits this. "I am certain I have not a right feeling towards Women—at this moment I am striving to be just to them but I cannot . . . Is it because they fall so far beneath my Boyish imagination?" When he was in school, he envisioned a "fair Woman" as a "pure Goddess." He realizes that this idealizing is unfair; he has no right to "expect more than their reality." Still, he can't stop, and this leads to a problem. He imagines women in all of their purity to be more sensitive to evil thoughts than men, and he fears that he might inadvertently offend one. Thus, he tries not to think insulting thoughts in feminine company. But his efforts yield the opposite: in trying not to think negatively, he does just that. He is afraid to speak, for fear of revealing his thoughts and so offending; he is also fearful of not speaking, because his silence might prove insulting. No wonder he is "in a hurry to be gone" when women are around.

His "perversity," he believes, arises from his "being disappointed since Boyhood." The biggest calamity of his adolescence was the death of his mother. In her place, he has constructed an ideal female, the "fair Woman a Pure Goddess," whom he worships, whom he lost. Projecting this image onto real, non-maternal women, he either envisions them as ghostly exemplars of his abstract standard, or as fleshly violations of perfection, corrupt.

Characteristically, charmingly, Keats swerves from this serious analysis, not very helpful anyway, to self-effacing humor. He could go on with his cogitations on women, but will leave off and hope for "better and more worthy dispositions" in the future. But even if affairs remain the same, he is content, for he is confident that he is really "wronging no one"—not because of his own behavior but because of women's indifference toward it. What woman really cares whether "Mister John Keats five feet high likes them or not?"

But this little joke might actually hide another root of Keats's woman troubles: his diminutive stature. In an age when the average male height was around 5'5", Keats's five feet wasn't as aberrantly short as it would be now. Still, Wordsworth at 5'10" would have towered over him, and he was shorter than the 5'2" Napoleon, whose name has become synonymous with the insecurities of smaller man. Keats felt his smallness, and assumed, so it seems, that women viewed him as less than a proper man. His notorious pugnacity overcompensated for his stature.

Whatever the cause, Keats in the summer of 1818 lacked confidence, and experience, when it came to women. Up until this time, he had likely enjoyed only one minor flirtation, with Isabella Jones, whom he had met in May or June 1817, while on a brief excursion to Hastings.

When Keats returned from his northern travels in August, he was in no shape to resolve his woman muddles. The cold he had caught on Mull continued to plague him. A toothache compounded his woes. He was anxious over Tom, who had grown much worse, and for whom he was again caring. The heavy nursing chores once more kept Keats from his writing, throwing him into a "continual fever" over his unproductiveness. He admitted that he had lost his "self-possession and magnanimity."

But candidates for romance suddenly pressed upon him. On September 22, he admits to Reynolds that "the voice and the shape of a woman has haunted [him] these two days." He is not in love with her, and actually sees her as a drain on his imagination. He is proud to say that poetry has won out this particular morning and has saved him "from a new strange and threatening sorrow."

Why sorrow and not pleasure? Probably because the woman preoccupying him is likely to break his heart. Her name, as he reports to George and Georgiana some two weeks later, is Jane Cox. When he met her at the house of the Reynolds sisters, he found her fascinating, with a "rich eastern look," "fine eyes[,] and fine manner." The secret to her attractiveness was her self-possession. Comfortable with herself, she put him at ease. But her "life and animation" calmed him, too, and continue to: "I forget myself entirely because I live in her."

Jane is too regal to inspire his love, though. He is content to enjoy from a distance her "magnetic power." This ardent admiration is intensely sensual ("she is a fine thing speaking in a worldly way") but doesn't

compromise his "*sensations.*" He can enjoy her erotic charge without succumbing to lust or worship.

This vision of Jane shows Keats in perfect equilibrium, stoked in body,
cool in mind. He has overcome his earlier worries over her, expressed in
the letter to Reynolds, and has admirably discovered a more fulfilling way
to relate to a woman.

A few weeks later, Keats had another opportunity to gain confidence,
this time with Isabella Jones, the woman he had earlier romanced in
Hastings. As he tells George and Georgiana, he and Isabella ran into each
other in the street, and he became her escort. As they walked, Keats won-
dered if their flirtation might be renewed. He wanted this but wasn't sure
she did. He had been in this situation before with her—she had "always
been an enigma"—and so accepted that he wouldn't be able quite to figure her out. The best he could do was "be prepared to meet any surprise."
Once they reached her home, she invited him up to her sitting room. After
some awkward moments, Keats made his move. Since he had "warmed
with her and kissed her" in Hastings, he thought it would be odd "not to
do so again." He tried. She "shrunk from it," though in "good taste," "not
in a prudish way." Keats claims that he found more pleasure in her gentle
rejection than he would have from a kiss.

It's hard to take Keats's nonchalance over this rebuff seriously. It's also
difficult to believe that he has no "libidinous thought about [Isabella],"
that he sees her as an intellectual companion. His subsequent remarks on
women, his most negative yet, suggest that he was hurt by her rejection
and that he doesn't really find her, or any other eligible woman, worthy
of companionship.

After his account of this incident, Keats envisions his future. Foremost,
perhaps protesting too much, he says will never marry: "Though the most
beautiful Creature were waiting for me at the end of a Journey or a Walk;
though the Carpet were of Silk, the Curtains of the morning Clouds;
the chairs and Sofa stuffed with Cygnet's down; the food Manna, the
Wine beyond Claret, the Window opening on Winander mere, I should
not feel—or rather my Happiness would not be so fine, as my Solitude
is sublime." No matter how wonderful the women—and note here that
Keats imagines her virtues in the most idealized terms—he would rather
have "sublimity to welcome him [home]": "The roaring of the wind is
my wife and the Stars through the window pane are my Children. The
mighty abstract Idea I have of Beauty in all things stifles the more divided
and minute domestic happiness—an amiable wife and sweet Children I
contemplate as a part of that Beauty, but I must have a thousand of those
beautiful particles to fill up my heart."

We can trust that Keats, so ready to greet the world's beauties, is sincere: nature has moved him, so far in his life, much more powerfully than have women (and nature won't reject him). But it's not only nature that surpasses wife and child; his imagination does as well: "I feel more and more every day, as my imagination strengthens, that I do not live in this world alone but in a thousand worlds—No sooner am I alone than shapes of epic greatness are stationed around me, and serve my Spirit the office which is equivalent to a King's bodyguard." It makes sense that Keats would revel in the fecundity of his imagination, and also in its obedience. (He can control it in a way he would never manage a wife.) What is strange, though, is Keats calling his imagination a bodyguard that defends his spirit against the outside world. This reduction of his normally yea-saying imagination to a "do not enter" sign: the opposite of negative capability, egolessness, disinterest, entering bravely the third room, sending the eye leaping.

Keats's next claim is more shocking. It's not only nature and his imagination that will keep him from a comparatively boring marriage. It's also that women "appear to [Keats] as children to whom [he] would rather give a sugar-plum than [his] time."

In this one letter to George and Georgiana, covering October 14–31, Keats goes from a confident, healthy vision of Jane Cox, to a somewhat confused account of Isabella Jones, to insulting all women.

Chapter 11

✦

Working Salvation

"I feel more and more every day, as my imagination strengthens, that I do not live in this world alone but in a thousand worlds." Keats needed to say this on October 31 of 1818, his twenty-third birthday. He needed, terribly, to believe it, too, because his potential for a satisfying life was dwindling fast. He had determined not to marry, and he had dismissed women from his serious attention. With Tom dying and George in America, he would soon be bereft of his brothers. His own ailments were curtailing his activities and portending more painful torments. He had little money, and more poverty loomed. Almost as agonizing as these morbid omens: the press savaged his epic.

The scathing reviews of *Endymion*, though he had expected them (knowing that his affiliation with Hunt would incite conservative attacks), could not have come at a worse time. The *Blackwood's* reviewer attacked the man more than the verse: "It is a better and a wiser thing to be a starved apothecary than a starved poet; so back to the shop, Mr. John, back to the 'plaster, pills, and ointment boxes,' &c."[1] The *Quarterly Review* did go after the poetry, calling it "more unintelligible [than Hunt's], almost as rugged, twice as diffuse, and ten times more tiresome and absurd than his prototype."[2] *The British Critic* censured the poem's lasciviousness: "We will not disgust our readers by retailing to them the artifices of vicious refinement, by which, under the semblance of 'slippery blisses, twinkling eyes, soft completion of faces, and smooth excess of hands,' [Keats] would palm upon the unsuspicious and the innocent, imagination better adapted to the stews."[3]

Keats had every reason to sink into self-pity. But he appeared to rally, once again displaying his admirable resilience. In an early October letter to his publisher Hessey, he proclaims that the reviews impacted him little. Blame, as well as praise, "has but a momentary effect on the man whose love of beauty in the abstract makes him a severe critic on his own Works." "My own domestic criticism," he continues, "has given me pain

without comparison beyond what Blackwood or the Quarterly could possibly inflict. And also when I feel I am right, no external praise can give me
such a glow as my own solitary reperception & ratification of what is fine."
He admits that the "slipshod" *Endymion* certainly deserves criticism. But
the poem could not have been otherwise, given his capabilities at the time
he wrote it: "It is as good as I had the power to make it—by myself—Had I
been nervous about its being a perfect piece, & with that view asked advice,
& trembled over every page, it would not have been written; for it is not in
my nature to fumble—I will write independently.—I have written independently *without Judgment*—I may write independently *& with judgment*
hereafter." Only by following his own vision, regardless of consequences,
could he discover his own genius: "The Genius of Poetry must work out
its own salvation in a man: It cannot be matured by law & precept, but
by sensation & watchfulness in itself—That which is creative must create itself." Courageously ignoring those, like Shelley, who told him not to
publish while young, and instead following the light of his own intense
senses: he leaped into *Endymion*, as he would "headlong into the sea," and
thus has become more knowledgeable about poetry's "soundings," "quick-
sands," and "rocks" than if he had written less ambitiously—had remained
on the "green shore," where men make tea and play "silly pipe[s]."

This letter looks back to his "life as a mansion" epistle of the prior
spring, which also hails plunging bravely into the unknown. But this present sequence differs from the earlier formulation: where May's analogy,
composed before Keats's northern trip, was mainly speculative, theo-
retical, this October vision, emerging from acute suffering, is experience
based, seasoned, hard earned. The imagery marks the distinction. The
mansion is secure; the ocean, engulfing.

The sea-plunging is not just colorful metaphor. It is method, a version
of the "leap of the eye" Keats extolled on Ben Nevis: the projecting of
sight, physical and cognitive, into inscrutable spaces where its failure to
perceive finality is precisely what generates its growths. This perceptual
and conceptual leaping is how the "creative" "creates itself"—by constantly transcending itself, ironizing its current position, revealing this
position to be necessarily limited in such a mysterious world, but also a
platform for a new jump into the unfathomable. This leaping is the work
of "salvation," life overcoming death.

✦

The day following this affirmative missive to Hessey, October 27, Keats
still had the redemptive powers of poetry on his mind. Writing to Richard

Woodhouse, a friend, he meditated more specifically on the "genius of poetry." He returns to the language he used in November of the year before, when he claimed that the poetic genius has no determined character but rather blends with whatever he perceives. Having been through a lifetime of anguish and doubt since then, Keats emphasizes the difficulty of determining to be undetermined. The "poetical Character," he begins, stands in opposition to the "wordsworthian or egotistical sublime," based on the notion that the poet is a stable "I" to which the world conforms. A true poet has "no self": "it is every thing and nothing—It has no character—it enjoys light and shade; it lives in gusto, be it foul or fair, high or low, rich or poor, mean or elevated—It has as much delight in conceiving an Iago as an Imogen." This "chameleon" poet delights in "what shocks the virtuous philosopher," relishing the dark sides of life as much as the bright—immune, if he so chooses, from the ill effects of the former, or the good results of the latter, because his goal is not action but "speculation." Distributing his being throughout his environment, he fades to nothing in particular, and so becomes, in lacking discrete identity, "the most unpoetical of any thing."

But this constant transference from self to other doesn't occur of its own accord. The poet generates the transmutation by "continually . . . filling some other Body." The poet must actively throw himself onto the object he perceives, and then "fill" it, imagining its interiors with such specificity that he metamorphoses into the object.

This jump is essential for powerful poetry, but it is psychologically risky. As Keats admits to Woodhouse, he is often "wretched" when he loses himself in others, because their identities so "press" upon him that he is "annihilated." Empty of being, he has trouble mustering a point of view from which to write poetry. If he is everyone else, who is he? Who authors the verse?

In a bracing move—and a prime example of Romantic irony—Keats, somewhat comically, wonders if the ideas he's writing to Woodhouse are even his. Perhaps the writing originated "some characters in whose soul [he] now live[s]." How can he even be sure if he is writing this sentence about not being sure who is writing the sentence?

Is it I who am writing these words, right now? After reading this letter, I wonder, and then wonder who's wondering, and so on. How to get work done in this vertigo? That's Keats's real question throughout the letter: how to create in the face of such potentially consuming ambiguity? If an anemic imagination can cause temporary writer's block, an overabundant one, capable of inhabiting whatever it fancies, can be paralyzing, too, perhaps more so, generating only endlessly self-regarding questions: who is who is who?

Take Coleridge, Hamlet of Highgate, whose brain was at least as teeming as Keats's. Every idea or object toward which the older poet directed his attention expanded or contracted, according to his imaginative whim. A crocus in his yard could inflate into the theory of photosynthesis, which itself could symbolize all organic life, which in turn could allegorize eternal spirit, and on and on, each new analogy adding another circle, wider, to the concentric rippling. Coleridge frequently gazed entranced at his mind's baroque circling, unable to manage anything other than scribbling in his notebooks approximations of the magnifying designs, or taking opium to shut down the riveting but bloated mental movie—a habit that actually conjured even more grotesque pictures, and so intensified his lassitude.

◆

What kept Keats from becoming Coleridge, an indolent addict, alternating between the mechanistically repetitive hunger for the next fix (of dope, of dream, of metaphysics) and the disintegrative hurly-burly of the high, when anything can become anything? His ability to balance repetition (the ideas over which he obsessed) and difference (thoughts ever novel).

Each major moment in Keats's development so far has been a response to his earliest great insight, expressed in the sonnet on Homer: powerful poetry and productive living arise from the interplay between the delighted stare and the wild surmise. The poem explores what happens during an empathetic experience of profundity: when the gap between poet and world closes, and he senses with quiet astonishment that he is somehow inside of what he perceives, and it, in his center.

But the satisfying wonder doesn't last for long; "enough" is so brief, in a life that demands "more." There is always more to know about the object. So the poet's joyful gaze expands into the explorer's turbulent speculation. But the surmises over the significance of inscrutable seas falter. This failure, though, is productive: the imagination strains harder to chart the waves.

But cultivating the "more" is exhausting. The mind needs to sink once more into the "enough." Then we grow restless with the rest, and once more yearn for better, and then grow tired, and take off once more, and so on.

This distinction between stare and surmise oversimplifies life: we almost never feel fully one way or the other, but both at once, or neither. Nonetheless, these two moods do seem essential, in some combination, for creating powerful art, which results from an interaction between the impulse to go with the flow and the push to organize the flux. In this exchange, the potentially harmful excesses of both sides are tempered, and the virtues thrive: sensual experience, potentially indolent, galvanizes; abstract thought, prone to suspiciousness, harmonizes.

Keats sought this dynamic median with increasing intensity as he struggled to avoid the debilitating extremes of lethargy and anxiety. His efforts to locate himself near the middle of this spectrum consumed him from this October of 1818 until his death. He returned to the gamut repeatedly, each time attempting to deepen and refine his understanding of its complexities and nuances. His active attention to the spectrum was precisely what saved him from falling off either end.

Keats focuses on this spectrum most fervently during times of crisis, developing the areas most pertinent to his situation. The fruitful interaction between stare and surmise in the Homer sonnet dissolves quickly. As Keats drafts *Endymion*, he seeks metaphysical certainty. He soon understands, however, that this quest incites constant anxiety. He pushes to the other extreme: passive acceptance of inevitable uncertainty.

This is late November and early December of 1817, the time of the letter on negative capability. Then, after a bleak winter and spring in Devonshire, during which Keats suffered a numbing depression, he commits to the kind of travel that can produce knowledge—not metaphysical, but more immediate, sensual knowing. This knowledge, he suspects, will not offer certainty, security; instead, it will prove mysterious, troubling. Keats trusts that the distress will generate wisdom, and that this wisdom will inform more powerful poetry.

These faiths he pronounces in May 1818, in the "life-as-mansion" epistle. By the time he reaches Mull, portents of his death chill him into another depressive funk. He accepts this ominousness. But his passivity is active: he projects his eye into the abyss where it perpetually explores, creates. In this moment, sometime in July, he returns to the spectrum's middle: between embrace of what is and striving for what might be. He has refined, though, his comprehension of each pole. An authentic gaze at existence doesn't bring delight but sorrow, since life kills what we love. And surmises about experience result in paralyzing confusion.

When Keats reaches October, he once more studies the relationship between acceptance and striving. His condition is now even more painful than it was in Mull. With his actual possibilities shrinking, he desperately needs the expansion of his imagination. He flings his mind out indiscriminately, hoping to enjoy more intensely the delights of empathetic apprehension. But he now realizes the dangers of living too vicariously. In the poet gone totally chameleon, no one is there, no one to surmise or to create.

What will Keats do next? We can imagine that he'll avoid "going Coleridge," bogged down in fruitless cogitation over his inability to establish an autonomous ego. But he won't avoid Coleridge's lassitude by simply ignoring the problem. He will look at it—this ongoing conundrum over how self and other relate—from a fresh angle, one based on his current state. This is the shape of all urgent knowing.

What drives this interplay between continuity and change—the repeating of the same question (what is identity?) and the creation of the new answer (identity is this, right now)—is existential need: the hunger for answers that will give shape, significance, and power to an individual life. This is pragmatic knowing, understanding what you need to live, not merely for knowledge for knowledge's sake.

No insight is true once and for all, but some are "truer" than others: those that enable us to live richer, fuller, more meaningful and beautiful lives. For Keats, what is true is what empowers him to perceive and create beauty, activities that turn out to be essential for him in his struggle against debilitating despair. The "truths" had to grow more and more powerful—that is, capacious, explanatory, and energizing—as his life became increasingly threatened by depression. An inverse proportion emerges: as his mental and physical health diminished, his "truths"—his interpretations, his manipulations of the amplitudes on the spectrum running between stare and surmise—became more sublime.

Chapter 12

Hyperion

During the somber autumn of 1818, Keats forced his imagination to breathe, to counter Tom's suffocating sickness: "His identity presses upon me so all day that I am obliged to go out—and although I intended to have given some time to study alone I am obliged to write, and plunge into abstract images to ease myself of his countenance his voice and feebleness—so that I live now in a continual fever—it must be poisonous to life although I feel well. Imagine 'the hateful siege of contraries'—if I think of fame of poetry it seems a crime to me, and yet I must do so or suffer."

Keats began the poem that eased his suffering in mid-September. Like *Paradise Lost*—the primary model for the work—*Hyperion* opens on mighty beings lying stunned in a dark underworld. They are the Titans, recently hurled from heaven by the Zeus-led Olympians. Saturn, the Titans' leader and former king of the universe, is now powerless in Tartarus, without a throne.

> Deep in the shady sadness of a vale
> Far sunken from the healthy breath of morn,
> Far from the fiery noon, and eve's one star,
> Sat gray-hair'd Saturn, quiet as a stone,
> Still as the silence round about his lair;
> Forest on forest hung about his head
> Like cloud on cloud. No stir of air was there,
> Not so much life as on a summer's day
> Robs not one light seed from the feather'd grass,
> But where the dead leaf fell, there did it rest.
> A stream went voiceless by, still deadened more
> By reason of his fallen divinity
> Spreading a shade: the Naiad 'mid her reeds
> Press'd her cold finger closer to her lips.

This scene is Keats's equivalent to Milton's "darkness visible": "non-existence existing." Things *are* in this world, but there is no meaningful motion or sound: stasis, silence only. Living time—growth and decay, success and failure—is absent.

This paralysis was threatening Keats as he wrote the passage. Like the depressed Saturn, he felt trapped in his own hellish environment, where he measured his days by absence: of his own achievement, of Tom's vitality. Most likely, he most felt the *lack* of feeling—just as does the broken Titan king, who lies upon the "sodden ground," with his "old right hand . . . nerveless, listless, dead, / Unsceptred," and his "realmless eyes" closed.

When Saturn does open his "faded eyes" to see his "kingdom gone," and the "gloom and sorrow of the place," he asks, "Who had power / To make me desolate? whence came the strength?" And how was this strength "nurtur'd to such bursting forth, / While Fate seem'd strangled in my nervous grasp?" Bereft of power, his "real self" now hovers somewhere between "the throne" and "earth."

The poem explores this question—more Hamlet-like than Satanic—that so vexes Saturn (and Keats in his October letter to Woodhouse): who's there? To view the work from a more Miltonic or Shakespearean perspective is to witness several different characters indirectly pose this question: Saturn, Oceanus, Clymene, Enceladeus; Hyperion, and the newly born Olympian, Apollo. Each character wonders: why did this overthrow occur, and what does it say about me? On the surface, the poem is a series of Shakespearean speeches occurring in a Miltonic cosmos.

But by the time we reach the work's conclusion—Apollo awakening—we encounter a rather different poetic world, a Wordsworthian one, centered on the evolution of a particular consciousness. This shift invites us to consider the entire poem alternatively: not as a traditional narrative with discrete characters but as a more modern quest for individuality. When we view the poem thus, from a more "Romantic" perspective (think *The Prelude*, or Blake's *Milton* and Shelley's *Prometheus Unbound*), each character becomes a component of one consciousness at war with itself, sick, struggling toward health, toward harmony. To understand the work as one poet's evolving interior is not to discount the more literal levels of significance. *Hyperion* is a "psychotopography": events are simultaneously "physical," palpable actualities within the fabricated world, and "mental," symbols of faculties in a particular fictional person's mind.[1]

Whose mind? The temptation is to say, Keats's. But since biographical criticism is problematic, a reduction of multitudinous literature to one personal history, the safest answer to the question is: the psyche is that of an ideal poet (like Blake's Albion or Shelley's Prometheus) here fallen asunder but striving to restore his creative powers. Nevertheless, the self represented by the characters in *Hyperion* illuminates Keats's vexed identity during the fall of 1818.

The ideal poet—the Poet, hereafter—begins the poem as Saturn, in despair, unsure of who he is, what he can do. He is most confused over his creative powers, his capacity as a cosmic poet: "Cannot I form? Cannot I fashion forth / Another world, another universe . . . ?" These vehement inquiries arouse the other Titans, laid low on Tartarus's floor.

While the vanquished muster, the poem shifts to Hyperion, the only Titan not yet fallen. He retains his rule over the sun. He is that part of the Poet's mind that has not yet fallen into despair, that still holds creative potential. Still, he is troubled. Why is he, used to bliss, now so "distraught"? Will he, too, fall? No. He will "advance a terrible right arm" over "the fiery frontier of [his] realms," terrify Zeus the "infant thunderer," and "bid old Saturn take his throne again." Even though he has just completed his daily course, he decides to mount his solar chariot and rush flaming toward Olympus. But even he can't alter time's fixed course. The "sacred seasons might not be disturb'd." His steeds will not take off. Unused to bending, Hyperion is "phrenzied with new woes."

If he is the sun-god but doesn't really control the sun, then is he really the sun-god? If he doesn't have agency over the sun, then does he have agency over anything? When he acts, is it he doing the acting, or something or someone else? Is he simply an organ in a massive inscrutable being, or a cog in some unaccountable machine? Can he ever know one way or the other?

With these questions weighing on him, and so on the Poet, Hyperion descends to Tartarus, where the Titans—like the fallen angels in *Paradise Lost*—are considering what to do. Book 2 opens with Saturn confessing to the assembly that his prodigious learning has not revealed to him the cause of their fall. He further acknowledges the seeming hopelessness of their condition. How to break out of this baffled paralysis?

Oceanus urges the company to accept their plight, for it was cosmic destiny that put them here. That all is fated is comforting, he argues, because it means that the fall of the Titans has nothing to do with their abilities. Why struggle? Celebrate. Just as the Titans were superior to the gods they overthrew, so the deities replacing the Titans will be better than they are. Oceanus knows. He has seen Poseidon, the new sea god, and is stunned by his power and beauty.

Clymene follows Oceanus, praising Apollo, Hyperion's replacement, in ravished tones. Before her exile to Tartarus, she heard, while wandering on the shore, a "new blissful golden melody."

A living death was in each gush of sounds,
Each family of rapturous hurried notes,
That fell, one after one, yet all at once,
Like pearl beads dropping sudden from their string:
And then another, then another strain,
Each like a dove leaving its olive perch,
With music wing'd instead of silent plumes,
To hover round my head, and make me sick
Of joy and grief at once.

This is a different kind of solar deity, as different from Hyperion as
Wordsworth is from Milton. Hyperion is regal, mighty, vigorous, suffused
with light, disdainful of doubt and sorrow, bellicose. Apollo—at least
in his music—is melancholy as much as joyful, attuned to connections
between death and vitality, suffering and beauty, melancholy and ecstasy.

Enceladus scoffs at Clymene and Oceanus. He is angry, craves revenge,
and asserts his freedom. Hyperion descends. The Titans try to rally, but
their war cries are "hollow."

Book 2 ends. The Poet, like the Titans, hovers in limbo, caught, like
Keats, between affirming destiny—he is dying—and asserting auton-
omy—he can live forever in original verse. Which extreme approaches
the truth?

◆

This dichotomy is wearisome. For the rest of one's days, one could vacillate between contentment and consternation, now valuing the "is,"
now celebrating the "ought." The polarities are too crude to describe the
mercurial nuances of a person's life, which encompasses far more than
the conflict or concord of freedom and fate, empathy and aloofness. To
chop into two, or three, or even sixty, a particular existence, is reductive,
simplistic. Moreover, fixating on a given polarity to explain life stunts
the imagination, confining it to an endless two-step at worst—this or
that, that or that—and a perpetual three-step at best: this related to that
results in something else, a this-that or a that-this. Such three-steps seem
profound, capable of capturing the paradoxical nature of life, in which
ostensible oppositions are always intrinsically related (think Hegel).
These formulas do offer attractive alternatives to clunky dualistic visions,
getting closer than "either/or" systems to the persistent "both/and-ness"
of experience. But as appealing as they are, these triads barely approach
the crushing plurality of life.

The Poet of *Hyperion*, attuned to these concerns, abruptly breaks with his broodings in the first two books: "Thus in alternate uproar and sad peace, / Amazed were those Titans utterly. / O leave them, Muse! O leave them to their woes." The true muse, he asserts, is too "weak to sing such tumults dire: / A solitary sorrow befits / Thy lips, and antheming a lonely grief." What seems a weakness—the inability to represent in verse the surmises and stares of the mighty Titans—is a strength, a propensity for poeticizing a phenomenon much more complex and important than mythological contestants: the ephemeral woe of one person. Interestingly, the Poet doesn't ask his Muse to understand this grief. He requests that she, through her music, celebrate the passing earth, regardless of its gloom.

> Flush every thing that hath a vermeil hue,
> Let the rose glow intense and warm the air,
> And let the clouds of even and of morn
> Float in voluptuous fleeces o'er the hills;
> Let the red wine within the goblet boil,
> Cold as a bubbling well; let faint-lipp'd shells,
> On sands, or in great deeps, vermilion turn
> Through all their labyrinths; and let the maid
> Blush keenly, as with some warm kiss surpris'd.
> Chief isle of the embowered Cyclades,
> Rejoice, O Delos, with thine olives green,
> And poplars, and lawn-shading palms, and beech,
> In which the Zephyr breathes the loudest song,
> And hazels thick, dark-stemm'd beneath the shade.

"Flush" all beings, although they are already glistening, with silvery life. Acknowledge the luminousness of the rose, and its undulating emanations. Allow also the morning and evening clouds to drift luxuriously, and the wine to bubble, and the involute shells to shine amidst the ribbed sands and liquid abysses. Let as well the young woman blush.

Note that each of these activities is rapid, nebulous. Things suffusing and being suffused; colors glowing; respirations streaming; vapors drifting; liquid bubbling; shells, strewn on wavy sands, glinting; a woman's cheeks turning amorously crimson. These motions express the "verbness" of existence, its constant transitioning from one state to another, in varying degrees of speed, ranging from nanoseconds to eons. There are no nouns, static identities to which one can point and say, "this, and no more." All "thises" are already, the minute you gesture, "thats."

Why would the Poet enjoin his Muse to encourage the moments that emphatically elude artistic description? Perhaps because the earth, at its vaguest, is most itself—when it reveals in pronounced form what is true all the time, as a flash of lightning reminds us that all matter is electricity, or a funeral recalls that every breath is a death-gasp.

Nothing is stable; nothing, knowable. This is what happens, and it is good. Such is *Hyperion*'s strange introduction to Apollo, the new sun god, who is weeping on the shore of Delos at the exact moment Hyperion, the outgoing one, glowers over dark Tartarus. Apollo is crying "bright tears" over the "murmurous noise of waves"—another revelation of the earth's ungraspable quickness—when Mnemosyne, the Muse, appears.

✦

The young god asks Mnemosyne if he has seen her in his dreams. She says yes, and that it was she who left the lyre at his side. He played it upon waking, and she and the rest of the universe "listen'd in pain and pleasure at the birth / Of such new tuneful wonder." Why, she inquires, does he weep, being so gifted? His reply, given that he is the potent god of light, is surprising.

> For me, dark, dark,
> And painful vile oblivion seals my eyes:
> I strive to search wherefore I am so sad,
> Until a melancholy numbs my limbs;
> And then upon the grass I sit, and moan,
> Like one who once had wings.—O why should I
> Feel curs'd and thwarted, when the liegeless air
> Yields to my step aspirant? why should I
> Spurn the green turf as hateful to my feet?
> Goddess benign, point forth some unknown thing:
> Are there not other regions than this isle?
> What are the stars? There is the sun, the sun!
> And the most patient brilliance of the moon!
> And stars by thousands! Point me out the way
> To any one particular beauteous star,
> And I will flit into it with my lyre,
> And make its silvery splendour pant with bliss.

He can't find the exact source of his sadness, and this failure makes him more sorrowful. But he does have some sense, however undefined, of the origin of his woe. He feels a gap between his aspirations and his situation, as a bird now grounded but with a memory of flight still (as an ailing eagle pining for the sky). This rift is all the worse because he is *not* grounded. The air yields to his step; he can walk in the ether. Why, then, does he hate this world that he can seemingly shape to fit his dreams? Because he can't know this world fully—its stars, the sun, the moon—and suspects that there are other worlds entirely that he hasn't even yet begun to know. He is desperate to grasp all existence and "flit into it" with his "lyre" and "make its silvery splendor pant with bliss." How can he fly into the "cloudy thunder" and know and make ecstatic its power?

Apollo pleads for Mnemosyne to help him understand this "aching ignorance" and overcome the woe. Then, straining to understand her mute face, he comprehends: "Knowledge enormous makes a God of me."

> Names, deeds, gray legends, dire events, rebellions,
> Majesties, sovran voices, agonies,
> Creations and destroyings, all at once
> Pour into the wide hollows of my brain,
> And deify me, as if some blithe wine
> Or bright elixir peerless I had drunk,
> And so become immortal.

The pain is a sign of his divinity, not a mark of his falling short of godhood, for a god is a being whose head is so inundated by knowledge that he can't contain all of the flow, much less organize it. The perpetual, forceful influx is intoxicating. The universe is overabundant with things to know, and he will never get to the end of it. The incompleteness is what is deifying, the perpetual space, just a sliver, between curiosity and satiation.

His epiphany is violent, a tendon-ripping jerk from one identity—"I am sad, just like a mortal, because I can't understand everything"—to another, radically different one: "My melancholy betokens my godliness, my almost infinite mind yearning incessantly for an infinity it can come close to but never grasp." "Wild commotions" shake him, make him "flush," just like the vermillion creatures the Poet earlier asked his Muse to engorge. He struggles like someone

> at the gate of death,
> Or liker still to one who should take leave
> Of pale immortal death, and with a pang
> As hot as death's is chill, with fierce convulse
> Die into life. . . .

Apollo's melancholy diverges markedly from the despair of Saturn. The Titan suffered a paralyzing depression, bereft of all possibilities save two unsatisfying ones—either submit to a hated victor or strive to overthrow him. The Olympian's sorrow is generative, opening to innumerable potentials for existence, yearning to realize as many as possible, though aware—and here the sadness—that the cosmos is beyond his apprehension.

We have already seen how the fallen Titans symbolize various energies of the questing Poet's psyche. What are Mnemosyne and her protégé to this Poet? They mark a new way of seeing and creating, one that avoids the crudities of the Titans and proves more sensitive to the radically varied ephemera of experience. Closer to life's precipitous flushes, the Poet resoundingly says "yes" to what is and what might be.

What's the point of celebrating what's happening anyway, saying to the rose, "glow?" This amounts to cheerleading. "The flower is red: Yay!" However, in a briskly inscrutable, "verbed" world in which there are no nouns to slow the flux, to cheer the process along, so indifferent to desires for security and clarity, is difficult. We usually endure or loathe. But we find ourselves once more back in the Titan's plight—hurt silently or rebelliously bellow. To move beyond this impasse, we must set aside our yen to understand and control, and cultivate a counter-urge: simply to *experience*, to ride, enjoy the rush rushing.

In *Rime of the Ancient Mariner*, Coleridge, before he slid into opium limbo, explored this sort of circulation. In the early sections, the Mariner, like Saturn, finds himself stuck and sorrowful: mired in a whitish hell in the unmapped Antarctic. What to do? Accept or rebel. He opposes, but he has so few options for action in his icy, befogged prison, that he can only muster a bowshot at an albatross, a wispy white synecdoche of the whole snowy antipodes. He kills the bird, the ice splits, and out he sails into hot southern seas. But soon the old sailor writhes for his crime. He watches his crew die, and stares at their rotting corpses for seven days, while lost at sea. His pain subsides when he unaccountably "blesses" the sea snakes he earlier hated. He celebrates their glistening eddies—not for their meaning but their flashing "tracks of shining white."

Coleridge realized this same process, in a more ordinary situation, in "This Lime-Tree Bower My Prison," in which his speaker is constrained to a bower (a foot injury) while his friends go hiking. He initially feels isolated from them and the natural scenes they'll enjoy. But he imagines what they're seeing, and what they're feeling, and he is no longer solitary. He watches a rook fly overhead, and, assuming that it will reach his friends, blesses it. It beats in the same beautiful air Charles now breathes.

Keats in *Hyperion* doesn't use the term "bless" to describe how the Poet relates to nature's fluxes, but this Poet's glorifying of these flows, his wishing them well, praising their energy and beauty, qualifies. In lauding these virtues, he *consents* to them—feels with them—and so, in a way, participates, emotionally running along beside them, eager to support them, push them along. He wants only to experience the currents as intensely as possible.

The grammatical mood most suitable for blessing—and Keats's Poet employs it—is the imperative, both command and exhortation. This duality is expressed perfectly by God's first utterance: "Let there be light." Exist! But also: Please allow this to happen. Similarly, Keats's Poet requests that his Muse "let" nature's undulations be—order them to exist, encourage them to occur.

It takes almost a godlike energy to affirm the intractable, deadly earth, really to honor it, not just say, "Ok," or "why not?," but "*Yes*." Keats's Apollo suggests that few are capable of this: only those poets who can "flit" with their music into the inscrutable amplitudes of the universe— stars, the moon, the sun, the thunder, regions not yet known—and make these powers "pant with bliss."

This idea of flying into an event on the strength of one's art and animating the event with bliss: this is not a mere poetic conceit. Apollo is describing what happens to objects artistically rendered. They seem to become more themselves, put their best energies forward, as though they *wish* to be turned into art. This isn't to attribute agency to things; it is to describe how art makes its subjects appear.

Think of Van Gogh's *A Pair of Shoes*. Unpainted, these shoes would be taken for granted, viewed as crude, mud-colored foot covers. But when Van Gogh portrays them, they come to life, revealing their useful history; they are integral to one farmer's life, ready to rise to their essential task, anticipating the feet that will sink into them.

Turn to cinema. A river, brownish, flowing over rusted cans and splotched with rotting paper, of sewage reeking: this is repulsive. Then Andrei Tarkovsky films this water—for a movie called *Stalker*—and it grows gorgeous, a dreamy repository of lost histories.

The eyes of Van Gogh and Tarkovsky: these "flit," respectively, into shoes and river, make them "pant with bliss": beautiful. The artist's seeing can transform anything, no matter how horrific. Lucian Freud's *Benefits Supervisor Sleeping* comes to mind, as does Tod Browning's *Freaks*.

Recall Keats's notion: intensity of gaze differentiates great art from good or poor. Those artists with the most intense stares see more than the rest of us, more complexity, nuance, depth. The gaze gains more compelling texture by the medium expressing it: paint, film, language. But the intensity isn't only optical, 20/20 vision. It is also emotional, based on strong, varied feelings toward the subjects: wonder toward the aura; sorrow over the passing; the frustration of incomplete understanding; amazement over the intricacy; hope for the essence of it; despair over the not getting.

With our perceptions dulled by habit and our feelings by convention, most of us merely perceive what we're told we should (the sun up there looks like a coin in the sky) and feel what our society dictates (that orb symbolizes life). Lacking the "enlarged & Numerous senses" of artists—to use Blake's descriptors—we miss the rush, and danger, of immediate, particular, idiosyncratic experience, which might well reveal the sun as it appeared to Blake, as an "innumerable company of the Heavenly host crying Holy Holy Holy is the Lord God Almighty," and so inspire mind-altering awe.[2]

Seeing not "with" the eye, but "thro it":[3] this is Blake's formula for mixture of optics and emotion that empowers the artist to "flit" into the subject of his focus and make it "pant with bliss." But we shouldn't forget: for Apollo, as well as for Keats (for Blake, too, beset with "nervous fear"), this yea-saying is so painful that it feels like death: dying into life. To accomplish this flitting, one must indeed die every second: let go of his solacing notions of himself and the world, leap into the nebulousness, celebrate the crazed flux, try to empathize with it, to depict it. But expiring, we stand most alive, witnessing with all of our hearts the world in a grain of sand, a host of daffodils, sinuous water snakes, Fingal's Cave.

✦

In spite of myself, I have had my blessings.

When she is four, Una and I are in a neighborhood park on a morning in May; we espy a mole burrow just where the grass fades into a weedy creek bank, and say in unison, "Look, look!" Another evening, more recently—she is ten—she and I take an evening run, and she asks, "Can I choose the route?" and I say "Yes," and she leaps onto a rock wall adjacent the sidewalk, runs on edge, laughing like a deranged fairy. And one afternoon in August I watch her sit in her reading chair, a window's beam flashing on her face, and she gazes up, stares at nothing, squints, looks sad, and returns to her page.

In instances like these, arising unpredictably as lightning, I am shivered, undeservedly, into a sense of what is—galvanic weird becoming unconnected with what I expect and what I fear, up-gushings like the ones to which Keats consented and thus sanctified.

These eruptions are rare because most of the time I'm trying to get Una to conform to my expectations of what an ideal child should be, holding up standards of etiquette, attention, cognition, diligence almost impossible for her, or anyone, to reach.

We are in the Keats house in Hampstead. I expect her to awaken to the verse. She wants to play in the heath. I am frustrated, cross. "You're missing out on an experience of a lifetime," I say to myself, not "she is more Keats now than I will ever be, with her delighted stare." In Rome, we visit the Borghese Gallery. I have prepared a lecture on Caravaggio's *Madonna of the Palafrenieri*. As I speak, learnedly (I imagine), her eyes wander up into the vast Renaissance spaces. I think only, "she's not taking full advantage of this experience," when I could also muse, "if spirit exists, she is now it."

So terribly hard, getting out of the way of yourself to get in the way of the world, especially when you are a parent, more especially when you are a father enamored of his own mind. Hence practices such as Zen, emptying the mind of fear and desire, opening it to nothing in particular and everything at once.

Fullness, shining, of the universe. Keats, as robust in his ruddy time as a young Orson Welles, minus the arrogance, would have made a terrible monk, Zen or otherwise. But his commitment to art turned him mystic, becoming nothing to sanctify all. I find his more exuberant sensuality much more amenable to my spirit than I do asceticism.

The enthusiasm, though, is not just energy; it is a form, a method, a kind of Zen after all. Keats's disciplined empathy—his commitment to negative capability, the leap of the eye, flitting in—elevates the act of blessing from mere chance to not improbable occurrence. And in his rigor—rigor in the name of elasticity—is the hope for me, that with more pragmatic focus, I might more frequently shed my narcissism, to communion open.

Play deliberate games, such as the one Emerson describes in *Nature*—if you want to understand the perception's power to shape experience, take in a familiar scene bent over, with your head hanging between your legs. A Keatsian stratagem: walk over and stand beside the person you perceive. I sense Una's boredom. I position myself beside her, look from where she's looking. I still don't quite empathize, but I'm closer. Another: imagine how both you and what you're experiencing would appear to another person, one positioned right over there, by the mulberry tree. Again, I would enjoy a different take on my daughter's malaise, perhaps note: I *am* pretty boring. Less casually: imagine myself (and this is hard given the bigness of my head) inside my daughter's brain (or in the whorls of the tree, or the strokes of Caravaggio's brush) and there, in that different place, absorb colors, textures, feelings, thoughts, afflictions, joys.

For someone isolated, these aren't silly sports. They can do, when I am in earnest, what good spiritual practice does: defamiliarize the familiar, undo habits, shock into apocalypse.

If the blessings of Keats can empower me to achieve such a revelation just once, I am sanctified, because if I can do it once, I can, potentially, undertake it sextillion times. I won't, being weak, but in the knowing is hope, which for the despairing is a kind of mercy.

Chapter 13

Fanny

Meshing form with content, Keats breaks *Hyperion* off a few lines after describing Apollo's transformation from known to unknown, life limited to boundless death. The god doesn't know what's coming next, can't know, and he convulses before the terrific multitude. Honoring this, Keats the Poet becomes inarticulate as well: "At length / Apollo shriek'd;—and lo! from all his limb / Celestial . . . ." Leaving the poem undone was an appropriate completion.

This shriek might well be the ecstatic outburst of Apollo, and so of the Poet, as he stands excitedly on the edge of the abyss. The shriek could also be meaningless scream before the monstrous. This second possibility suggests an alternative reason for the poem's abrupt end: John Keats was horrified by what happened on December 1. Tom died. After this date, Keats wrote *Hyperion* no longer.

Keats clearly had Apollo's awakening on his mind, though, during the winter of 1819. In the two notable poems he did write—"Why Did I Laugh Tonight" and *The Eve of St. Agnes*—he explored the relationship between the shriek's contraries: giddy affirmation, terrified "no." He needed the solace of his new wisdom, for his spirits remained low. In addition to mourning Tom, he was still battling his "Morbid Temperament," chronic sore throat, and anxieties over money. The woman question continued to hound him as well—consume him, really, for he was falling in love with Fanny Brawne.

When Keats returned from his summer walking tour, he visited the Dilke family at their home in Hampstead, Wentworth Place. The family was living in one side of the duplex property. The other was owned by Brown, who had let his space for the summer to the Brawne family, composed of a widowed mother and her three children, Fanny, eighteen; Samuel, fourteen; and Margaret, nine. Exhausted by his trip, ill, worried about Tom, Keats barely acknowledged these lodgers, though they were surely mentioned by the Dilkes, with whom the Brawnes had become friends.

While Keats was settling into Well Walk to nurse Tom, the Brawnes, with Brown needing the rooms once more for himself, moved to Elm Cottage, on Devonshire Hill, only a brief walk from Wentworth. The family continued to visit the Dilkes throughout the fall, where they almost certainly heard kind words spoken of Keats. They probably met the dejected young poet during one of their visits, in the middle of November, when Keats was seeking refuge from the sickroom at the home of his old friends.

Fanny remembered. She found Keats's "conversation . . . in the highest degree interesting and his spirits good, excepting at moments when anxiety regarding his brother's health dejected them."[1] This first contact made little impression on Keats, however, so perturbed was he. We learn of his early impressions of Fanny later, starting on December 16.

These first descriptions are part of a long letter to George and Georgiana, spanning from mid-December to early January. Keats reports Tom's death to his brother—"the last days of poor Tom were of the most distressing nature; but his last moments were not so painful, and his very last was without a pang"—and announces his plans to move in with Brown at Wentworth. Not far into the letter, he mentions the family who had rented Brown's home over summer, and singles out the oldest daughter: she "is I think beautiful and elegant, graceful, silly, fashionable and strange we have a little tiff now and then—and she behaves a little better." Two days later, he describes her more fully:

> Shall I give you Miss Brawn[e]? She is about my height—with a fine style of countenance of the lengthen'd sort—she wants sentiment in every feature—she manages to make her hair look well—her nostrils are fine—though a little painful—he[r] mouth is bad and good— he[r] Profil is better than her full-face which indeed is not full put [for but] pale and thin without showing any bone—Her shape is very graceful and so are her movements—her Arms are good her hands badish—her feet tolerable—she is not seventeen—but she is ignorant—monstrous in her behavior flying out in all directions, calling people such names—that I was forced lately to make use of the term *Minx*—this is no[t] from any innate vice but from a penchant she has for acting stylishly.

After Keats's anemic, rather neurotic portraits of Jane Cox and Isabella Jones, this forthrightness is refreshing. Here is a full person, complicated and conflicted. She is beautiful, elegant, and graceful, but also silly, superficial. Her countenance is fine, but she lacks expression. He likes her hair. He also likes her nostrils, but finds them unattractive as well. Her arms

are good, her hands bad. Her mouth: good and bad. Keats finds her ignorant, but is also fascinated by her "penchant for acting stylishly."

The key adjective is "strange." In the months prior to this encounter
with Fanny, Keats had used the word in two important contexts, both
times to signify a phenomenon dangerous and wonderful. In late July, in
one of his travel letters to Tom, he had written that "the western coast of
Scotland is a most strange place." Notably, this sentence follows closely
his description of Fingal's Cave as a bizarre Titanic temple, and sums up
his entire experience of Scotland's west as a land of deadly yet invigorating mist. Two months later, in a letter to Reynolds, Keats once more
employs "strange," this time in describing Jane: she is "a new strange and
threatening sorrow" from which he has thankfully escaped. The connection between Scotland's foggy shores and Jane Cox's perilous seductions
is not far-fetched. Both coast and Cox are to Keats terrae incognitae.

In these cases, "strange" makes the unfamiliar, familiar, wrenching
the truly outlandish into a concept—the strange—at least somewhat
comforting. In the case of Fanny, however, this dynamic is reversed:
the word transforms a seemingly quotidian eighteen-year-old girl into
something marvelous. In light of the last pages of Hyperion, this shift is
understandable. The phenomena Apollo blesses are not grand, distant,
extraordinary (like mythic Titans or Fingal's Cave), but more common,
intimate, expected—a girl blushing, the aura of the rose. The ordinariness
of these energies, however, is illusory. Blushes and multi-foliate crimsons
are routine only to lazy eyes, guided by the long-ingrained Platonic habit
of emphasizing the general over the particular. Such perceptual inclina-
tions seek the Girl Blushing behind the specific embarrassment of one
teenaged girl, named Fanny, on Friday, December 15, wearing a powder-
blue smock and chartreuse shawl and standing in the center of a candlelit
room. To the more intense gaze, that of an interested painter or poet, each
instant a cheek reddens is potentially fascinating. If she decides to transform her experience of a particular instant into a portrait or a poem, and
if she is skilled, she will illuminate the moment's singularity, reveal the
unfamiliar in the familiar, and startle her audience into a fresh, enlivening
experience of what they must have witnessed hundreds of times before.

This discussion of the implied poetics of Keats's initial impression of
the woman with whom he soon fell in love is ridiculous. People don't live
theoretically, "apply" "principles" discovered in "art" to their everyday
lives. Keats saw Fanny, found her interesting, had his curiosity aroused,
became infatuated, and groped, in a letter not intended for publication,
toward an initial assessment of her virtues and flaws, in which he rather
casually threw out the word "strange."

It is salutary, when trying to discover the patterns of a life, to remember: so much is whimsical. "Strange" could just as easily have been "curious," or "interesting." Still, there are recurring structures in anyone's life, and they usually express a consistent drift. So, even if Keats's description of Fanny is capricious, it nonetheless does connect, in its attention to the concrete, to a theme that was much on Keats's mind during the winter and spring of 1819: the relationship between real and the ideal.

Chapter 14

Suicide

In a late February letter to George and Georgiana, Keats writes of Bailey's insulting behavior to one of Reynolds's sisters, Marian. Bailey was romantically interested in her, but expressed his feelings tepidly. Marian didn't return his affections, though she valued him as she would a brother. After falling precipitously in love with another woman, Bailey renounced Marian. He returned her letters, and asked for his. This behavior hurt Marian, angered her family and friends, including Keats. From this unpleasant affair, Keats concludes that a person's extreme statements are often attempts to hide an opposing principle to which he is secretly committed. Bailey ridiculed romance, but turned out to be the most romantic of men. In the same way, someone who slights women probably loves them, and "he who talks of roasting a Man alive would not do it when it came to the push."

Don't take everything literally. It is shallow to do so in a world where everyone is duplicitous at the very least, if not triple or quadruple or centuple or infinite. A worthy man, Keats continues, understands the complexity of behavior. In fact, his worth is inseparable from this deeper comprehension: knowing that all events are multilayered, with the layers often at odds with themselves, he strives toward awareness of his own variety, and cultivates richer heterogeneity. He aspires to make his life, as we have already seen, a "continual allegory," his outward actions connoting diverse meanings. His life is a "Mystery . . . like the scriptures, figurative—which such people [shallow literalists] can no more make out than they can the hebrew Bible."

This is not a typical definition of allegory, usually viewed as a narrative whose characters, settings, and events represent abstract ideas. Everyman is everyman. The Red Cross Knight is Holiness. In Keats's passage, allegory is closer to symbol, as Goethe defines it: a "true symbolism is where the particular represents the more general, not as dream or shadow, but as a living momentary revelation of the inscrutable." To live allegorically, in this regard, one must realize that each particular moment, perceived with imagination—with sensitivity to nuance, ambiguity, lubricity—is ultimately inscrutable: not meaningless, but extravagant in meaning. Comprehending this fact, one generally acknowledges his own multiplicities, celebrates his exuberant messiness.

Shakespeare, called by Coleridge "myriad-minded," exemplified allegorical living. So Keats thought. Keats bases his conclusion on the plays, deeply attuned to the riddles of life, and generously disposed toward them, usually depicting monomaniacal types as villains (Iago) or victims (Othello), and alternatively showing more flexible, open-minded characters as heroes, successes (Rosalind in *As You Like It*, Prospero in *The Tempest*).

In contrast to this "figurative" man is the one, like Byron, who simply "cuts a figure," who exists according to preset conventions—*this* is how to be a dandy, or a rebel. He is as shallow as the worst literalist, ignoring his fecund complexities in favor of conforming to comforting rules.

Was Keats in his earlier takes on the feminine merely cutting a "figure," rehearsing the tired misogynistic conventions of his time? Is Keats now, in detailing the complexity of Fanny, "figurative," alert to riddles in himself and others? It appears so. In renouncing philosophy for being overly abstract, Keats in a March 19 letter claims that "nothing ever becomes real till it is experienced—Even a Proverb is no proverb to you till your Life has illustrated it." Sensation, not thought, is the path to the real. The ideals set forth in parables—moral, aesthetic, or otherwise—are worthless until they connect with actual experience, inform it, enrich it. This confluence is rare: the gap between the lessons of parables and the muddledness of life is wide.

Keats dramatizes his efforts to heal this rift in a sonnet he includes only a few lines later, which begins, "Why did I laugh tonight?" He tries to answer. First he considers the extremes of metaphysical parables and myths—gods and demons—but finds no solution. Perhaps his "human heart" will solve the riddle. No. He asks the question again. Still no answer: only "mortal pain" and "darkness." The sestet poses the question a third time. He doesn't answer but asserts, "I know this being's lease / My fancy to its utmost blisses spreads." The being appears to be himself; the lease, the amount of time he is allotted to live. But though this existence is finite, closer each second to expiration, it nonetheless expands his fancy to extreme joy. Is the bliss legitimate? Fancy is sometimes a synonym for imagination. It could be that the poet's finite existence stokes his imagination to create beauty. But fancy also hints at the adjective "fanciful." Is the bliss fantastical, superficial, trifling, illusory? The final lines imply that the answer is "yes."

Yet could I on this very midnight cease,
And the world's gaudy ensigns see in shreds.
Verse, fame and Beauty are intense indeed
But Death intenser—Death is Life's high mead.

If the poet could die this very night (the "could" says that he might actually wish to) and so see how insignificant worldly activity really is—nothing but gaudy flags, fanciful, fantastic, showy, ostentatious—then he would realize that the poet's typical pursuits are not as powerful as death. It is death, not art, that is life's greatest reward.

This poem looks back to "When I Have Fears," another meditation on how life's finitude inspires the pursuit of fame and beauty. But where that earlier poem concludes with a rather lucid message—the quest for poetic fame and idealized romance blinds us to life's possibilities—this one is disturbingly ambiguous throughout.

We can safely say that the poem express the difficulty of pursuing knowledge in a hopelessly lubricious world, where the lessons of parables, with their heavens and hells, only occasionally mesh with actual experience. But if metaphysical myths can't answer the poem's question about laughter, imagination and poetry can't either. Fancy might be able to create enduring blisses in the face of transient existence, but these pleasures, when one is on the verge of death, are but vulgar banners. If neither philosophy nor poetry can satisfy our longings for solace, what can? An intense experience of death. This interpretation of death might be another invocation of the memento mori theme—remember death to take life seriously. But given the poem's nervousness, its desperation—it repeats the same question three times, and the poet seems to be laughing rather maniacally throughout—its vision of death seems edgier than a comfortable Renaissance motif. The poet probably means that in a world where there is so much uncertainty, so much that poetry and philosophy can't alleviate it, death is the only certainty.

The poem is about the thirst for knowledge, and its quenching only in death. This is the meaning that Keats urges on George and Georgiana, assuring them that the poem isn't about his desire to kill himself. But George should be concerned for his brother, for Keats can only know this one knowable thing by dying. And this death is life's true reward, the only way to escape the agony of living. Suicide is desirable.

This is the first appearance of a theme that will haunt Keats's poetry from now on: the seduction of suicide. There had been hints of a suicide obsession earlier. Death wishes whisper in the sonnet on the Elgin Marbles; and Keats dedicated *Endymion* to Thomas Chatterton, who committed suicide at the age of eighteen. But self-murder presses in the winter of 1819 and pushes until Keats actually tries to kill himself in the weeks before tuberculosis does it for him. When he writes to Fanny Brawne the next winter that he would "as soon think of choosing to die as to part from" her, and when he follows this in August 1820 with a confession that he is sickened by the "brute world" and "should like to die," we can believe him.

Just on the level of philosophy—forgetting for a moment the poet's actual life—we can understand why suicide preoccupied Keats. Keats's leading question is: how to find solacing significance in a world without enduring meaning? His answer is usually: empathetically embrace the vitality of life and express this vitality in appropriately vigorous art. This activity creates aesthetic meaning: truth (this is how this experience is) beautified, beauty (this is how this experience shines), verified. But this saying of "yes" to a world painful and dark, whose only surety is that it destroys what we love, is extremely difficult, even in the best circumstances. When one is depressed or tired or bitter, it becomes almost impossible, and then, absent the activity of blessing, the world sinks to darkness and pain solely, loss and more loss. Then escape becomes desirable. There are drugs and alcohol and sleep for temporary liberation, suicide for permanent. If the choice is between bewildered suffering and painless stupefaction, the stupor seems logical. What is better: temporary or chronic numbness? Chronic. Keats turns Camus: suicide or not is the question.

Add to this line of thinking the drifts of Keats's own life—exhausted by physical and mental illness, agitated by fears of never marrying Fanny or achieving poetic fame—and we can understand the intimations of self-slaughter.

Chapter 15

✦

Dream and the Dragon World

The *Eve of St. Agnes*, the other significant poem Keats completed during this winter, a medieval romance evocative of pre-Raphaelite sensuousness, is a suicide note.

The poem, which Keats completed in February 1819, right around the time he was falling in love with Fanny, seems yet another variation on the "life is short, art is long" theme, with art in this case the vehicle by which young lovers achieve undying beauty, and life the force that kills. But the work is anything but—life is sure enough death, but art is, too.

The poem opens cinematically: an old Beadsman kneels in the bitter cold, counting his rosary. He rises, takes his lamp, returns—"meager, barefoot, wan"—to the chapel, and there shuffles among the "sculptur'd dead." He hears music's "golden tongue" from beyond a door leading from the church, but it doesn't cheer. He turns toward a pile of "rough ashes," where he sits all night grieving for sinners.

From this grim opening, the poem—as with a camera—tracks to the music, to a "glowing" party celebrating St. Agnes's Eve, January 20, a night, so the superstition goes, on which a young maiden, if she performs certain rituals, will dream of her future husband. The gathering flutters with the plumes and jewelry of youthful revelry. At the center of the gaiety is beautiful young Madeline, by numerous suitors sought. She is preoccupied, though, with the ceremonies required for her marital vision: eating no supper before bed; lying supine while wearing white; not looking anywhere but upwards before falling asleep. So consumed is she that she doesn't hear the music, strangely described as "yearning like a God in pain."

These initial stanzas establish the poem's contraries: old age, coldness, death, mournful prayers, versus youth, warmth, life, and celebratory music. Is there an art that can marry these antinomies, both integral parts of life? Keats hints that there is when he describes the party's music as a longing like a pained God. The language recalls Apollo's awakening in *Hyperion*: a "dying into life," necessary for the poetry the god aspires to write, sensitive to life's rush toward death, but capable of rendering the destruction beautiful. This sort of verse is a possibility in *The Eve of St. Agnes*. The potential is not realized.

Porphyro replaces Apollo. He is Madeline's young lover, and wants to see her. But since his family is feuding with Madeline's, he must sneak into the castle and meet her secretly. Stealing inside, he encounters Angela, Madeline's nurse, sympathetic to the "star-crossed" lovers. She helps Porphyro gain entrance into Madeline's bedroom. There he hopes to win her hand in marriage—not, he convinces the nurse, seduce the maid.

So begins one of Keats's most bizarre sequences, voyeuristically erotic in spite of Porphyro's stated design. Hidden in a closet, he watches Madeline unclothe before going to bed, gazes upon her "empty dress," and listens to her breathe. Once she is asleep, he ventures to her bedside, and there sets up one of the most wondrous dessert tables of all time, loaded with "a heap / Of candied apple, quince, and plum, and gourd"; with "jellies soother than the creamy curd, / And lucent syrops, tinct with cinnamon"; and finally with "Manna and dates, in argosy transferr'd / From Fez; and spiced dainties, every one, / From silken Samarcand to cedar'd Lebanon." After laying out these sweets, substitutes for the parts of himself he would offer for Madeline's delectation, he tries to rouse her with soft words, before vaguely threatening to get in bed with her if she doesn't open her eyes. When she doesn't comply, he plays on a lute "an ancient ditty, 'La belle dame sans mercy.'"

The song stirs her, but she's not sure she's awake. All she feels is the pain of being trapped between blissful dreams and unpleasant life. She sadly tells Porphyro she heard him singing in her dream and witnessed his eyes as "spiritual and clear." Now, however, seeing him in the flesh, she views those same eyes as "sad," and his overall mien as "pallid, chill, and drear." So cadaverous is he in comparison to his phantom, that she fears he is dying. She begs him not to. Porphyro accommodates.

> Beyond a mortal man impassion'd far
> At these voluptuous accents, he arose
> Ethereal, flush'd, and like a throbbing star
> Seen mid the sapphire heaven's deep repose;
> Into her dream he melted, as the rose
> Blendeth its odour with the violet,—
> Solution sweet. . . .

Has Porphyro, engorged with his passion and throbbing, entered Madeline, mixed his fluids with hers, literally ending her virginity? Or has he turned "ethereal" and blended his spiritual body with her dream image, thus keeping her chaste? Or—and this is what the paradoxical language suggests most strongly—is Porphyro now somehow physical *and* spiritual, reality and dream?

These questions are difficult to answer, and Madeline is no help. After Porphyro assures her that he is no dream, and calls her his bride, she exclaims: "No dream, alas! alas! and woe is mine! / Porphyro will leave me here to fade and pine.— / Cruel! what traitor could thee hither bring?" These remarks suggest that her lover has indeed had sex with her, and not with her consent. But we could just as easily conclude that she is simply offended over his pretending to be a dream and entering inappropriately her bed.

Porphyro is no cad. He asks her to be his bride and follow him to his home over the "southern moors." The two will sneak by all the passed-out revelers and make their way under cover of the bad weather, "an elfin-storm from faery land, / Of haggard seeming." She agrees, and so they escape.

Here is where the poem, already weird, becomes outlandish. Thus far, it has appeared to be a tale of young lovers caught charmingly between lust and romance. But in detailing their escape, the poem hints that these two lovers might not have existed at all. In the dark, they "glide, like phantoms, into the wide hall; / Like phantoms, to the iron porch, they glide." No one notices these specter-like youths. The many bolts on the door "full easy slide," and the chains "lie silent on the footworn stones;— / The key turns, and the door upon its hinges groans." And the lovers are "gone." The poem shifts to past tense, as though the lovers actually are from a former age, not of this present moment at all: "aye, ages long ago / These lovers fled away into the storm."

It appears that the two didn't express their affection physically but married in dream only, and in dream continue to dwell. They never leave their little love-bower, apparently, but lie warmly enclosed while they move in a mental sphere. Or perhaps they never existed, but are ghosts from an old romance like "La belle dame sans mercy." Indeed, from the minute Porphyro sings this lay, the two lovers behave like phantoms.

Who can blame them? As Porphyro merges with Madeline's dream, the poet tells us that "meantime the frost-wind blows / Like Love's alarum pattering the sharp sleet / Against the window-panes." Porphyro himself is acutely aware of these treacherous conditions, reminding Madeline, just after his melding with her, that "tis dark: quick pattereth the flaw-blown sleet," and again, one line later, the same: it is dark, and "the iced gusts still rave and beat." As this storm ravages the earth, interior gusts assail particular bodies. Angela the nurse dies at poem's end, "palsy-twitch'd, with meagre face deformed," and the old Beadsman hurries toward his own death "among his ashes cold."

Porphyro as poet—singer of lays, maker of dreams—can't bless, flit into, and make blissful this monstrous world. His music is not that of a yearning god in pain, laboring to say "yes" to the tragic earth. Porphyro's art is "nay-saying," a negation of the physical with an eye toward that which is beyond suffering: dream. But dream, a gathering of ghosts, a realm beyond actual pain and pleasure, is death. To desire only dream, as Madeline and Porphyro do, is suicidal.

Keats connects dream and death in a sonnet he completed about two months later, in mid-April, called "On a Dream." Just as Hermes "took to his feathers light" after lulling Argus to sleep, so the poet, having with his pen hypnotized the "dragon-world," has "fled away." Is his charming of the monstrous world part of his dream, or is it the prelude to it, preparation for his flight? We can't know, but we can note the strangeness: a poet who is either already asleep or getting ready to sleep, puts the world to sleep. In his own particular slumber, the poet doesn't dreamily follow the path of Hermes. Instead of cruising to Ida or Tempe, he descends into the second circle of Dante's "sad Hell," where the lustful are doomed to whirl for eternity in rain and hail. There "lovers," already condemned to sadness, need not bother telling their sorrow. The poet then sees his own lover, kisses her pallid lips, and floats with her in the "melancholy storm."

Keats based this poem on an actual dream. In an April 16 letter to George and Georgiana—part of the same long letter containing "Why Did I Laugh"—he reported that he had been reading the fifth canto of the *Inferno*, in which Dante's Pilgrim meets Paulo and Francesca in the second circle, among the lustful. Upon hearing their woeful tale, the Pilgrim swoons in grief. Thinking of this canto when in a recent "low state of mind," Keats dreamed of descending to hell's second circle himself: "The dream was one of the most delightful enjoyments I ever had in my life—I floated above the whirling atmosphere as it is described with a beautiful figure to whose lips mine were joined at it seem'd for an age—and in the midst of all this cold and darkness I was warm—even flowery tree tops sprung up and we rested on them with the lightness of a cloud till the wind blew us away again—I tried a Sonnet upon it—there are fourteen lines but nothing of what I felt in it—o that I could dream it every night."

The dream here and in the sonnet is of being dead, but the dream death is pleasant, an escape from the "dragon-world" or a low "state of mind" to a realm exotically beautiful and forever warm. It would be surprising if Keats didn't have *The Eve of St. Agnes* in mind when detailing the dream.

When Porphyro and Madeline fade phantom-like from the castle, they flee from a world of "sleeping dragons." The atmosphere into which they escape is stormy yet they will remain warm.

Romance and sonnet, in offering dream as a suicidal escape from a horrendous world, predict the distinction between poet and dreamer in *The Fall of Hyperion: A Dream*, which Keats wrote in the late summer of 1819. The dreamer, "weak," is dissatisfied with life but won't try to improve it. He wants out. Escapist verse is his vehicle. But short of actual suicide, he can't get away. He becomes petulant, demeaning earth, pining for heaven. A "fever" unto himself, he poisons and vexes. In contrast, the poet seeks "no wonder but the human face" and "no music but a happy noted voice." He is "a sage; / A humanist, physician to all men." He "pours out a balm upon the world."

Chapter 16

Soul-Making

Call the world if you Please "The vale of Soul-making." Then you will find out the use of the world (I am speaking now in the highest terms for human nature admitting it to be immortal which I will here take for granted for the purpose of showing a thought which has struck me concerning it.) I say "*Soul making*" Soul as distinguished from an Intelligence—There may be intelligences or sparks of the divinity in millions—but they are not Souls till they acquire identities, till each one is personally itself. I[n]telligences are atoms of perception—they know and they see and they are pure, in short they are God—How then are Souls to be made? How then are these sparks which are God to have identity given them—so as ever to possess a bliss peculiar to each one's individual existence? I—How, but by the medium of a world like this? This point I sincerely wish to consider because I think it a grander system of salvation than the chrystiain religion—or rather it is a system of Spirit-creation—This is effected by three grand materials acting the one upon the other for a series of years. These three Materials are the *Intelligence*—the *human heart* (as distinguished from intelligence or Mind) and the *World* or *Elemental space* suited for the proper action of *Mind and Heart* on each other for the purpose of forming the *Soul* or *Intelligence destined to possess the sense of Identity*. I can scarcely express what I but dimly perceive—and yet I think I perceive it—that you may judge the more clearly I will put it in the most homely form possible—I will call the *world* a School instituted for the purpose of teaching little children to read—I will call the *human heart* the *horn Book* used in that School—and I will call the *Child able to read, the Soul* made from that school and its *hornbook*. Do you not see how necessary a World of Pains and troubles is to school an Intelligence and make it a Soul? A Place where the heart must feel and suffer in a thousand diverse ways! Not merely is the Heart a Hornbook, It is the Minds Bible, it is the Minds experience, it is the teat from which the Mind or intelligence sucks its identity. As various as the Lives of Men are—so various become their Souls, and thus does God make individual beings, Souls, Identical Souls of the Sparks of his own essence—This appears to me a faint sketch of a system of Salvation which does not affront our reason and humanity.

Keats wrote this on April 21, 1819, five days after composing "On a Dream." It renders with striking clarity the troubling mysteries over which he had been brooding, ranging from the necessity but virtual impossibility of blessing a painful, perplexing, evanescent world; to the seductions of suicide, all but irresistible, when the ability to bless falters; to a sort of escapist poetry that might serve as suicide's proxy. More importantly, however, this passage catalyzed Keats's waning imagination, awakening it from the doldrums of being unable to complete *Hyperion* to the sublimity of creating, in miraculously quick succession, the great odes.

Since setting aside *Hyperion* in early December, Keats was unable over the winter and spring to start another project he thought worthy of his poetic powers. The poems he was writing, such as "Why Did I Laugh," *The Eve of St. Agnes*, and "On a Dream" were bordering on dreamy nihilism. Keats himself was fading into a suicidal malaise. Where was the muse's grace?

On Tuesday, April 20, Keats and Brown had invited Taylor, Woodhouse, and Reynolds to dinner at Wentworth Place. Around nine, when the group had just settled into a game of cards, a storm struck, making the guests' respective journeys home unthinkable. The men decided to stay the night, and the game resumed. It lasted until morning. Just as the sun rose, Keats went to his room. But he couldn't sleep, and so took up the long letter he had been writing to the George Keatses.

He summarized his recent activities before breaking into his breeziness with an abrupt "Wednesday Evening"—this was April 21—followed by a complete draft of "La Belle Dame sans Merci," composed rapidly during the daylight hours. This was the most accomplished poem Keats had written in months. It expressed powerfully his recent insights and fears.

An unnamed speaker asks a "knight-at-arms," alone and pale in a wintry land, what "ails" him. The knight says he met a "lady in the meads," a beautiful, fairy-like creature, with long hair, lightsome step, and wild eyes. He found her irresistible, and courted her. He made her flowery garlands and bracelets, as well as a belt. In his mind, these gifts—note that they are all constraints—bound her to him. She looked at him as if she loved him. More definitely, she "made sweet moan." Was this pleasure or pain?

Convinced of the enigmatic woman's affection, the knight put her on his horse and rode with her all day long. She turned to him and sang a "faery's song." She offered him sweet roots, honey, and manna. In a language "strange," she again appeared to express her deep affection. Then she guided him to her "elfin grot," where she wept until he calmed her with four kisses. She lulled him to sleep. He dreamed of pallid warriors, princes, and kings, all apparently dead. In unison, they cried, "'La Belle Dame sans Merci / hath thee in thrall!'" The knight awoke to find himself alone and ill, and now loiters in a cold land.

The creature the knight encounters is mysterious. Instead of embracing her as a wondrous being that will not conform to his understanding, he constrains her with bracelets and a belt that might be painful, and puts her, perhaps against her will, onto his horse, and forces her to ride with him all day. Along the way, he construes her bizarre speech to mean that she loves him.

But a sliver of doubt remains. In the back of his mind, he suspects that she remains beyond his understanding and control. The dream suggests this. Even though the creature has not threatened him, the knight envisions her as a seductress who imprisons and sickens men like him.

When he awakens, he suffers the consequences of cognitive egotism: alienation, because he closes himself off from a world too inscrutable to solve; and sorrow, since his unreasonable expectations of intellectual security are constantly being undercut by actual experience.

In revealing these causes of isolation and depression, "La Belle Dame sans Merci" suggests how to achieve a life of connection and energy: do what the knight does not. Where he binds his beloved and construes her cryptic words to mean exactly what he wants, we might give those we love ample space in which to be what they wish and to speak until they get their intended meaning across.

Only a few hours after completing the poem, Keats imagined this more vital life: as soul-making. He returned to the Apollonian epiphany of Hyperion. But while Apollo's vision and Keats's soul analogy are similar in kind—both say "yes" to a life that says "no"—they differ in degree. When Apollo awakens, he leaps from the innocence of not quite knowing who he is and what he can do, to the experience of his godhead and immense potential. This jump is painful as well as pleasurable, killing the old to make way for the new, but more joyous in the end, since the transformation produces exhilarating hopes. Such is Apollo's "dying into life."

In his description of soul-making, Keats "lives into death." He is a long way from innocence. Having suffered through one loss after another, he feels his options dwindling, is more attuned to what he can't do—find happiness, live a long time, complete an epic, have the funds to marry—than to what he can. He is fully experienced, then—experience being increasing constriction. There is no "brave new world," but "been there, done that." Jaded, Keats's soul-making is more resigned than joyous, bent on reconciling to unchangeable pains. The movement is not upward and outward, as it was with Apollo, but downward, inward—toward the small scripts of the hurting earth, into the chambers of a contracting heart. Where Apollo's "yea" was to a "probably not," Keats says "yes" to a hard, angry "no way in hell."

Keats's more mature meditation is more pertinent to our adult lives, when we are not so much awakening as trying to stay awake. But though wizened, soul-making is more vitalizing than youth's flashes: the longer elation of finishing a marathon, as opposed to the rush of a mile sprint.

In order to make a soul, we must transcend our initial condition, as "intelligences." When we are intelligences, we are but "atoms of perception": unbiased, indifferent, objective, godlike perceivers, untarnished mirrors reflecting perfectly the objects nearby, or windows unstained, through which light particles pass unhindered. For most, this perceiving would be the acme, the lucid vision toward which one labors, scientifically, philosophically, artistically, all of one's life.

But this position is the nadir, opposite of soul. The problem with being an intelligence is that you are everyone and no one. What you see, everyone else sees, exactly, and vice versa. There is no difference, no identity, no distinct art or thought. To become a soul, an individual, you must distinguish yourself.

A soul arises from the interaction of three materials: an intelligence, a human heart (as distinct from intelligence, or mind), and the world, where mind and heart interact. The world is like a school designed to teach children to read; the heart is like the reading primer (or "hornbook") the school uses; an intelligence resembles a child who cannot yet read. The curriculum of this school is "pains and troubles." The heart as hornbook teaches the "thousand diverse ways" to suffer. The child who learns to read this book—who actively scrutinizes the world's pain, and genuinely absorbs these pains, as well as other forceful experiences—burgeons into a soul.

As an act of reading, soul-making requires that one turn symbols into meaning. For simple, non-literary texts (bland, straightforward experiences), this transformation is easy: the range of possible meanings is limited. But for more complicated literary pages (compelling, ambiguous encounters), the conversion of script to signification is difficult, since the meanings are myriad and often conflicting.

To be a good reader of literature, and so of complex, manifold, contra-dictory experiences, one must peruse empathetically, set aside his biases and theories, and project oneself into the book, the event. Negatively capable, one can enter more intimately into the text, the world, and gain a deeper understanding of its depths, than someone who fits the text into a prefabricated set of ideas, as Procrustes cut victims into his ghastly bed. Empathetic reading requires powerful imagination, ability to fling (to flit) the mind into page (the quick flushes and blushes of life). Among the turbulence, the mind must construct a map to help it navigate the multitudinous relationships, between and among the dark and the bright, depth and surface, the ironic and the literal, contradiction and paradox, and on and on. To remain enlightening, vital, useful, the map must change as the textual landscape changes, and so must be in a state of endless revi-sion. The goal of the map is to illuminate what is most powerful, most alive, most compelling, and most beautiful, in the text. Where the map becomes blind to these forces—by being too close (disappearing in the flow) or too far (overly general)—it loses utility.

To make a soul is to transform life into art, to face suffering honestly, with as much empathy as possible, while interpreting the pain so that it doesn't debilitate but empowers, becomes significant, instructive, beauti-ful. Soul-making, art-making is pragmatic, not true or false, but useful or not, solacing or not, intense or no.

John Dewey, an enthusiastic reader of Keats, illuminates this pragma-tism. Dewey defines experience as the interaction between a creature and its environment, in which the creature struggles to find equilibrium. This effort requires the creature to be aware of its needs and find ways to meet them. Its life is a battle between lack and fulfillment. The most intense experiences are those where the creature overcomes stiff resistance to achieve its goal.[1]

This interplay takes place on a biological level. But it can also occur on more complicated scales: creatures not only meeting their immedi-ate needs but also forging more durable equilibriums—useful habits or designs. Humans enjoy the rhythmical alternation between these more enduring concords and the disruptions of existence. The most interesting objects are the obstacles that invite this satisfying give-and-take. Artists deliberately reflect these rhythms in their works, creating especially com-pelling tensions that result in remarkably pleasurable resolutions. The artist's labor is never done: as self and environment change, needs and satisfactions alter, and so the artist—and indeed anyone fashioning a meaningful, invigorating life—must be attentive to new disunities, fresh harmonies.

The world wounds the heart, ripping it between desire and fulfillment. Soul-makers dwell in the gap, the heart's valley. Through it they
toil, bridging the torn walls. Poets, especially intense forgers of soul, are
experts at this healing work.

✦

If suffering is soul-work, then does degree of pain dictate the level of wisdom? Keats underwent terrible torment; his insight was prodigious. The
same can be said of Emerson, who lost his six-year-old son to scarlet fever,
and lost his first wife Ellen to tuberculosis after only a year and a half of
marriage. Other artists transmuting their intense suffering into knowledge:
Dickinson, Woolf, Berryman, Sexton, Primo Levi, to name only a very few.

Compared to these figures, I haven't suffered much. No one close to
me has died. I enjoy good physical health, a steady job, a decent salary.
True, my bipolar disorder has made my life difficult, at times extremely
difficult, but not unbearable.

Still, I have elevated my mental illness into the centerpiece of my life.
I persistently teach courses on the relationship between melancholy and
creativity. I have written three personal books on my depression, and two
academic studies on the psychology of gloom. I appear in the media from
time to time as the "guy who can talk about melancholy or disaster." I
identify with my depression, am *the depressed guy*.

But my ideas on the wisdom that can grow from suffering have not
arisen from my existential pain. They are borrowed from poets like Keats
and Shakespeare. And I have applied these ideas to my life poorly, falling
well short of the buoyancy, robustness, generosity, and creativity of Keats
or Emerson.

I am a poseur, performing more than living. What might crack the
façade, expose me to the real, whack me into discernment? Would it
take a catastrophe? If so, I'll take glum and benighted. Would the break-
through require a deeper understanding of Keats, Emerson, or Woolf? I
have reached the end of my intellect concerning these writers.

You could say that I have made, stoically, a virtue of necessity, turning
my genetic depression into a relative good, an inspiration to lecture and
write. But you could also say that I am weak, idle, lacking the strength to
forge my own tragic wisdom, or the gumption to read heroic poets more
insightfully.

The latter claim is more accurate. I am only a monad of perception. I
haven't shaped my suffering into an identity. I have foisted a borrowed
identity onto my sullenness. I am not Wilson, a particular hurting man

particularly schooled by his pain. I am tepidly Keats, a befogged mim-
icker of another.

Keats would say that Thomas à Kempis's *The Imitation of Christ* is
a blasphemous book. To copy the pattern of another, even if that other
is the God-Man himself, is to kill creativity, which is for Keats the sine
qua non of the spiritual life. And here I am composing, in my words and
gestures, *The Imitation of Keats.*

If you see Keats on the side of the road, kill him. Clever, maybe, to say;
harder to do. Foolish to do. You don't have to slay gurus to find your own
path. Better to walk with the teacher some miles down the way, until a
fork divides you, and you continue onward, carrying his good influence
as far as it goes.

Empathy goes two ways at once. I can imagine what it's like to be
Keats, which I have done to such an extreme that I often lose my sense
of what it's like to be Wilson. I can also envision what Keats would do, if
he and I were the same. What would Keats do if he were a husband and
father; if he were manic depressive; if he were not a genius, but moder-
ately intelligent and articulate?

The problem is balance: how to imagine myself into Keats without
losing my identity, and how to imagine Keats into me without leaving
the poet behind? Keats was able to do this, in grand terms, with Shakespeare and Milton, in lesser, with Hunt and Haydon. In fact, he was
able to achieve this double vision in a remarkable number of instances,
transforming beings into mirrors—I see myself in that "sea-shouldering
whale"—and windows—that whale sees through my eyes.

My daughter, whose presence most distinguishes me from the childless
Keats, is the marker of my wisdom or lack. Sometimes my love for her
is only suffering: love not as an embrace of her being, right here, right
now, but as fear of losing her, if not this minute, then later. I know that's
what a child does: leave her parents, first psychologically, shoving out
her parents' influence with her own identity, and then physically, leaving
home for college, for a spouse. This is of course how it should be, but
the fact of it seems tragic. To sorrow over this inevitable distancing, a
sorrow grown of the ache to keep her close, speeds the going. What child
wants to be around a father whose sole concern is to keep her attached
to him?

Selfish suffering: hurting because the world isn't exactly what you want
it to be, regardless of the desires of others. For this suffering, no remedy,
since the hunger for the world to conform to your egocentric ideal is
bound to go unsated. Such suffering is not soul-making; it lacks empathy,
resists growth, proves static, repetitive.

I have struggled with this sort of suffering, and not only in relation to my daughter but in relation to so many experiences, about which I inwardly lament—"This is passing, passing, gone, placeholder now only for lack, what I want but is not." More significant suffering, Keatsian, deemphasizes the "not," holds to the "is," is charitable toward it, tries to love it.

The Keatsian paradox, twofold: to hate transience, focusing only on its negations, is to speed it up, letting potentially significant moments pass without noticing them; to embrace the ephemeral, to hone in on its generative powers, is to slow time down, intensifying certain moments into aesthetic density. The inevitable suffering of the former—desiring what cannot be, time stopping—produces only more suffering: stronger desire, more painful disappointments. The equally unavoidable sorrow of the latter—the loss of what one loves—can create pleasure: more love to counter the losing.

Childless, and a perennial child in some ways himself—consumed by his orphaned status—Keats nonetheless mentors in parental wisdom, showing me that living fatherhood requires a full "yes" to the death of the same, that this dying is abundantly alive.

Chapter 17

✦

Psyche

Only days after Keats finished his passage on soul-making, the morbid transmuted to the miraculous, he began to explore, in his six odes, the pitfalls and ecstasies of living artistically, as well as the dire consequences if one fails to do so. Aside from "Ode to Psyche," finished by April 30, and "To Autumn," composed by September 19 (two days before a dejected Keats ate a nectarine), we don't know the chronological order of the odes. We can discern, though, a thematic development. "Ode to Psyche," "Ode on Indolence," "Ode on a Grecian Urn," "Ode on Melancholy," "Ode to a Nightingale," "To Autumn": taken in this order, the odes dramatize the journey from being a mere intelligence to learning to read the heart, or becoming a soul.

"Ode to Psyche" models the sort of reading Keats urges in his passage on soul-making. It is an overture, a primer, a hornbook.

Keats included the poem near the end of the long verse letter to George and Georgiana. The ode, he tells them, describes the appropriate worship of the last goddess of the Greek Pantheon. From Apuleius's *The Golden Ass*, Keats learned the myth. Psyche, the daughter of a king, is so beautiful that the people adore only her, to the neglect of Venus. Jealous, Venus decides to destroy the young woman. Her son Cupid falls in love with Psyche, however, and marries her. His only rule: when he visits her in the night, through an open window, leave off the light. One evening, though, she lights a candle, beholds the glorious god. He vanishes. She journeys to find her husband, constantly hindered by Venus's obstacles. Jove pities the melancholy beauty. He elevates her to godhead and reunites her with Cupid.

Keats's ode opens as would a prayer, asking Psyche—Greek for "soul"—to hear his "tuneless numbers." The poet then abruptly shifts, from addressing the goddess to talking to himself. He wonders if he really saw Psyche earlier that day, or if he dreamed his vision. Wandering through a forest "thoughtlessly," he witnessed "two fair creatures,

couched side by side," amid "hushed, cool-rooted flowers, fragrant-eyed, /
Blue, silver-white, and budded Tyrian." The two are Cupid and Psyche.
They are either on the verge of kissing or have just kissed.

Are we inside or outside the poet's head, in a dream or the actual? The
poet doesn't pause on this question in the next stanza but instead celebrates the goddess. He exclaims that though she was the "latest born" of
the Olympian deities, she is the "loveliest vision far." Yet there is no temple to honor her, nor are there altars, choirs (of virgins making "delicious
moan"), hymns, shrines, groves, oracles, or "pale-mouthed prophet[s]
dreaming." The poet volunteers to supply these vehicles of worship.

As Psyche's sole priest, he will construct in her honor a temple in some
"untrodden region" of his mind, where "branched thoughts, new grown
with pleasant pain, / Instead of pines shall murmur in the wind." These
mental trees will feather the mind's mountains, peaks becalmed by winds
and streams and birds and bees. In the midst of this landscape, the poet
will decorate his sanctuary

> With the wreath'd trellis of a working brain,
> With buds, and bells, and stars without a name,
> With all the gardener Fancy e'er could feign,
> Who breeding flowers, will never breed the same:
> And there shall be for thee all soft delight
> That shadowy thought can win,
> A bright torch, and a casement ope at night,
> To let the warm Love in!

The proper worship of the goddess who struggled through time's
destructions to discover lasting beauty is artistic striving. The poet
imagines the literary part of his brain as a latticework, through whose
diamond-shaped warp nature's growths—sensory data—perpetually
interweave. Cultivating the vigorous textures is "Fancy," whose fantasies
become real. Fancy "feigns," or imitates, the unnamed images and ideas
in his mind, fashioning artifices ever new, different. The inventions, like
Pygmalion's statue, come to life.

In this forest of the mind, the poet fashions his soul-shrine, a textile,
a weaving of the lines of life (stalks, tendrils, beams), as well as a text,
whose words function like things. This vital book expresses the vigorous
maker, the Gardener, a symbol for the poet at his best, when his fantasies, fresh and vivid, immediately manifest in living language. His mind
and his book, growing from his struggles to build out of the indifferent
valley an artistic identity, must, if they are to remain vibrant, continually

develop, interweaving lattice and growth, repetition and difference, "I am" and "I become."

Is any of this serious? Though the poem begins confidently, as an impassioned prayer, at the start of the fifth line, the poet questions whether Psyche is real or not. He might have dreamed her, and might well be dreaming throughout the poem. He never tells us he has awakened. Regardless, the shrine he builds to Psyche exists only in the unmapped recesses of his mind, and is no more than an artifice (a fantastical trellis) within an artifice (the fake forest).

How meaningful can such a reverie be? How about the poem itself, a trellis-work, originating in the poet's hypnagogic mind? The internal Gardener "feigns," fakes, deceives. The poet himself, the Gardener externalized, might be doing the same. What we have here is a sham religion devoted to a sham goddess who demands as her phony worship texts that fake life.

These ambiguities place us, the readers, in the same position as the poet. Just as he beholds a goddess who may or may not be a dream, so we experience a poem hovering between earnestness and fantasy. What does the poet do with his mysterious vision? He appreciates its beauty, which he converts into his art, the poem itself. His example invites us to imagine his poem the same way he treats his experience of Psyche—as a compelling mystery we can transform into creative interpretations, works of art.

Chapter 18

✦

Indolence

The two primary kinds of limbo are the limbo of paralysis, the inability to choose because all seems bleakly the same; and the limbo of readiness, openness to numerous possibilities at once, a kind of negative capability. How to turn the stasis of indifference into the charged calm of deliberate anticipation, curve the flat-line of chronic "no" into the expanding spiral of the "maybe," the "might," the "perhaps," the "possible"? "Ode on Indolence" answers.

After an epigraph from Matthew on how the lilies, unlike anxious humans, "toil not," "Ode on Indolence" opens with the poet witnessing three figures with "bowed necks, and joined hands, side-faced." Wearing sandals and white robes, they passed his gaze, one behind the other, as figures would on a turning marble urn. They then passed again, as if the urn were once more revolving. They were "strange" to him.

Before these shadows appeared, the poet was deep in morning-time languor, indifferent to pleasure and pain. He laments their appearance, since they upset his design: to lose his identity entirely, and so both agency and responsibility. Before they came, he was close to becoming a corpse, or, better, an empty space, not a subject upon which objects act. (The poet has already hinted at this fantasy in the poem's first line, constructed in passive voice, and so lacking an agent: "One morn before me were three figures seen.")

The poet's focus on repetition reflects his lassitude. The figures go round and round in stanza two, in perfectly regular turns. They do exactly the same in stanza three. Such predictability—suggesting stasis, death—is comforting to a man who wants total inertness.

In stanza three, the hypnotic pattern shatters. The shadows turned to face the poet, then faded away, and suddenly he "burn'd" to follow them, "ach'd for wings." He now knew them: Love, Ambition, and Poesy, with the last being the poet's greatest love. In fact, Poesy was his very "demon," which could be the evil, self-destructive part of himself, but more likely is his personal "daimon," his ameliorative inner voice. Whatever the demon's identity, Poetry has called the poet, who wished to be no one, a mere "intelligence," into particular being, a someone, who possesses an individual soul—a dark side, and a bright.

Creative power arises with this self's arousal: the ability to speak the phantoms, formerly filmy, indistinct, into clear and distinct beings. Whether these ghosts were real or not—out in space or in his head—is immaterial: what is important is the speaking of nothing into something. The poet in "Ode to Psyche" did the same, shaping his own vision—was it real or not?—into an exquisite trellis.

Once the indolent poet named the shadows, he ardently yearned for their nearness. But they faded just as he formed them. Bereft, angry, he immediately renounced them, as though suddenly consumed by that petulant feeling of "if I can't have them, I don't want them anyway." Love, he said, is undefinable and difficult to locate. Ambition originates from a "man's little heart's short fever-fit." And as for Poesy, his favorite: she can't provide "joy" as can a "drowsy noon" or an evening "steep'd in honied indolence." Better to ignore all three, and pursue what is most satisfying: total indolence.

How to return, though, to his peace? The poet tried what had worked before: repetition, simply for the sake of repetition. "A third time came they by," he claimed, repeating almost verbatim what he had earlier said. But the reiteration didn't work. Before he could settle into a nice monotonous rhythm, he grew vexed over why the three figures disturbed him in the first place.

> My sleep had been embroider'd with dim dreams;
> My soul had been a lawn besprinkled o'er
> With flowers, and stirring shades, and baffled beams:
> The morn was clouded, but no shower fell,
> Tho' in her lids hung the sweet tears of May;
> The open casement press'd a new-leav'd vine,
> Let in the budding warmth and throstle's lay;
> O Shadows! 'twas a time to bid farewell!
> Upon your skirts had fallen no tears of mine.

Earlier, the poet described himself as benumbed, half-dead, incapable of joy or sorrow, close to self-annihilation. The imagery he uses now, however, is vital. He was not in fact a void, but a "soul," active like a flowery lawn; or moving shadows; or rays of light. The weather enclosing this verdantly relaxed disposition was fittingly cloudy, conducive to fogginess and sleep, but the mists on the horizon were heavy with vernal water, and on the verge of releasing their nourishing drops. A nearby "casement" stood open, through which fecund warmth and birdsong flowed, a portal much like the unhinged window through which heated Cupid enters.

Even though the poet wishes the shadows had never come, they have enlivened his mind, making it much more attuned to organic energies than it was before, more keen on being (as opposed to nothingness), as well as much more imaginatively active, more likely to detail his psychological state in striking imagery than in bloodless abstractions.

The poet signals this more alert state in the final stanza, where he trades the past tense he has largely used heretofore for the present, and the indicative and interrogative moods for the imperative. He might still value indolence, but he is now a dynamic agent with faith in his words' conversionary powers.

He bids the "three ghosts" adieu. You can't stir my soul for long, he claims, you can't "raise / My head cool-bedded in the flowery grass," because I "would not be dieted with praise, / A pet-lamb in a sentimental farce." He chooses—and this is important for a poet who earlier wanted to make no decisions—*not* to be hungry for fame. This fortitude has turned him gentle. Not tempted by the three figures, he can wish them a tranquil journey. "Fade softly from my eyes," he tenderly commands, "and be once more / In masque-like figures on the dreamy urn." He has better things to do than obsess over these reveries, such as enjoy his "visions"— immediate, compelling, beautiful, decidedly not the "phantoms" he is now dismissing. These vivid sights will issue from his "idle spright," not his from his inert spirit, and be, no doubt, really something to behold.

This ode, which seems static—it ends where it began, in indolence—is in fact a conversion piece, depicting a poet's elevation from mere laziness to deliberate idleness. The difference is vast. Merely lazy, the poet without trying or thinking to try sinks into moribund lassitude. He is nothing more than a weak consciousness fading into oblivion, nearing the condition of an "intelligence." Then three figures float through his sleepy brain. He could simply let them go, and go blank. But he doesn't. He names them, giving to their airy nothingness shape, being, purpose, and then treats them as if they are alive. Doing so, he resembles the Gardener in "Ode to Psyche," whose imaginings come to life. By the time this indolent poet sends his imagined children away, he is ready to return to his lounging. However, now he cherishes another kind of indolence—tranquilly meditative, not simply lazy; cultivated, versus accidental. This intentional passivity is anticipatory limbo, in which he is alert, flexible, playing with possibilities.

Just as Keats's poet in the ode reaches this state—one that marks his move from a mere intelligence to the verge of soul-making—he not only tells the three phantoms to fade "softly away." He also commands them to "never more return!" Since the poem opens with an imaginary urn turning, shows the urn revolve two more times, and uses the same diction to describe the revolutions, the word "return" is charged. It hums back through the poem, impelling us to the beginning. We read the poem again, but with a more subtle idea of indolence in mind. The experience is not the same; it is richer, more intricate. We reach the end once more. Now our notion of indolence, based on a comparison of the two kinds of lassitude, is even more expansive. The "return" sends us to the beginning again, and we peruse once more, and so on, each time increasing comprehension.

This circumferential form of interpretation deepens and extends the reading practice encouraged by "Ode to Psyche." That poem, recall, encouraged readers to seize ambiguity—textual and otherwise—as an opportunity to interpret creatively. Here Keats refines the process: to empathize with the events we find most fascinating, we must turn the happenings around and around, altering our interpretations with each changing turn, but careful to maintain a degree of consistency. Too much repetition, nothing learned; too little, and nothing, again, learned.

Chapter 19

Urn

Like "Ode to Indolence," "Ode on a Grecian Urn" begins with the poet gazing at an urn, material in this case. He has traded dreams for reality: here is a marble artifice, and there are figures upon it. What do they mean?

Is the urn a solacing symbol of eternity, or an artifice divorced from earth's vitality? The first lines raise this question: "Thou still unravish'd bride of quietness, / Thou foster-child of silence and slow time." The urn, though married, remains (is "still") virginal, inviolate, pure. Pristine, unbothered by lust, perhaps even all desire, she is "still" on another level: utterly tranquil, unmoving, as though beyond time. She is beyond sound, too—quietness is her husband, silence, her foster parent—and so in another way outside of temporality, for she is not yet "tensed" by conjugated verbs. A-linguistic, she is in some fashion outside of space, as well, because she is not articulated into discrete units. Her non-material qualities explain her status as a foster-child: her true parents are not of this world; "silence" and "slow time," sympathetic to her virtues, take care of her in the true parents' absence.

But "unravish'd," the adjective that started this discussion, need not be positive. If we remember that "ravish" comes from the same root as "rapture," we realize that this urn, as personified, has not enjoyed ecstasy of any kind, is rather prudish. Her stillness is unproductive stasis. Her silence is muteness. And her indivisibility is bland. These limitations explain her foster-child status: she is an orphan or an outcast.

Is the urn good or bad, or somehow both together? Initially the answer seems clear: the urn is overwhelmingly positive, an ideal work of art, beautiful and true. It is a "Sylvan historian" who can, because it is eternal and pure, "express / A flowery tale more sweetly than our rhyme." What are the tales? "What leaf-fring'd legend haunts about [its] shape / Of deities or mortals, or of both, / In Tempe or the dales of Arcady?" Who are these gods and men? Who the "maidens loth," and what are they struggling to "escape"? "What wild ecstasy"?

Even though the poet doesn't know what mythological stories the urn is actually telling, he continues to praise it. He can't hear the music accompanying these painted tales, but no matter: while "heard melodies are sweet," those "unheard are sweeter" because they play not to the "sensual ear" but more endearingly "pipe to the spirit ditties of no tone." This kind of virtual music—suggested by images but emanating no actual sound waves—can play forever, since it requires no real musicians or instruments, and it can play perfectly, since there's no one to make a mistake, and it can fulfill whatever ideal of music the listener (not really hearing anything) imagines.

Also exquisite are the urn's figures—a musician, a tree, a lover close to kissing his beloved—who will never grow old or die. But is this lover really happy? We can't know. If the lover feels flush with erotic possibilities not yet tested and so pleasurably hopeful, then his situation is positive; but if he, like Tantalus, suffers from desire forever unfulfilled, then he is not in paradise but hell. The poet doesn't consider this dark possibility. He turns up the volume of his praise.

> Ah, happy, happy boughs! that cannot shed
>   Your leaves, nor ever bid the Spring adieu;
> And, happy melodist, unwearied,
>   Forever piping songs forever new;
> More happy love! more happy, happy love!
>   Forever warm and still to be enjoy'd,
>   Forever panting, and forever young;
> All breathing human passion far above,
>   That leaves a heart high-sorrowful and cloy'd,
>   A burning forehead, and a parching tongue.

He's already celebrated the eternal spring, the endless music, the un-aging lover. Why the repetition? And why the reiteration of the word "happy" six times? One could say that this poet is trying to convince himself, through fervid repetition, of what he suspects might not really be true: perhaps it isn't so wonderful to be stuck in the same position for centuries.

Perhaps becoming aware of this grimmer aspect of suspended animation, the poet turns to a somber scene: a priest leading a lowing heifer to a sacrifice. Though the animal is being pulled to a "green altar" and is dressed in "garlands"—all suggesting a vernal festiveness—she is obviously terrified and will soon be slaughtered. And while this slaughter, like most springtime sacrifices, is a religious ritual offering gratitude to the gods of rebirth, the killing also acknowledges life's painful interplay between life and death. The poet asks the urn who accompanies the priest to the sacrifice, but his inquiry lacks the excitement of those rushed questions of the first stanza. It doesn't seem rhetorical, either, as those earlier questions did (they really meant—*look at all this action!*); the question expresses real curiosity, maybe confusion or even forlornness, leading as it does to another, patently bleak question: "What little town by river or sea shore, / Or mountain-built with peaceful citadel, / Is emptied of this folk, this pious morn?" The poet doesn't know, but he does understand that this town is frozen in silence, and there is "not a soul to tell" why it is "desolate." This melancholy absence of sound differs markedly from the spiritual quietness of the urn's foster parent and its unheard music.

The poet's dynamic interpreting of the urn's mystery has led to an impasse. Though he began the ode somewhat ambiguously, he quickly became an advocate of the urn as a symbol of art's power to raise our gaze from decay to beautiful aloof shapes that inspire contemplation, ecstatic, of eternity. But in praising the urn's spiritual virtues, the poet sensed disturbances: to be paralyzed for eternity can be hell. Now, in considering the urn's capture of a tormented cow, he has lost his enthusiasm, and is back where he started. Is the urn positive or negative?

In the final stanza he tries to answer again.

> O Attic shape! Fair attitude! with brede
>   Of marble men and maidens overwrought,
> With forest branches and the trodden weed;
>   Thou, silent form, dost tease us out of thought
> As doth eternity. Cold Pastoral!
>   When old age shall this generation waste,
>   Thou shalt remain, in midst of other woe
> Than ours, a friend to man, to whom thou say'st,
>   "'Beauty is truth, truth beauty'—that is all
>   Ye know on earth, and all ye need to know."

The poet is so baffled he doesn't even know what he's looking at anymore. The urn is nebulous: a "shape," an "attitude." Then he regains his focus: the urn is ornate embroidery, teeming with people and greenery. This metaphor recalls the fecund trellis of the working brain: an artifice vital and tranquil at once, merging vigor of the earth with the more stable structures of the mind. The urn might be a symbol for the artistic brain. The poet projects onto the silent, unthinking, inanimate urn his lively thoughts and words, transforming it into a mirror of his artistic struggles. He desires an art that will elevate its subjects above transience, but he is aware that such an art, while attractive as a vision of eternity, is static, lifeless. This awareness hints at another ideal: art should be sensually attuned to the energies, though painful, of this breathing earth. Can the artist's mind reconcile motion and stasis, life and death? If the mind functions like a trellis it can. The mind as Grecian urn can bring these two drifts together, too, with the solid vase grounding lively images, and with the brisk pictures animating the unmoving marble.

The urn as symbol of an ideal artist's mind at work as well as of the kind of artifact such a mind might produce: the poet has apparently discovered how to turn the urn's stasis into a positive: a still backdrop highlighting the bright, quick crisscrosses. Why, then, doesn't he end his poem right here? Because he suspects that the urn's embroideries might actually be "overwrought," too studied, exaggerated. The ostensible concord between energy and form is perhaps only manic fantasy. (The same is possibly true of the trellis work.) If so, then the urn is likely to exhaust its viewers—make them overwrought—infecting them with unrealistic desires for unrealizable harmonies.

How else to explain the poet's abrupt criticism of the urn? It is now once more a "silent form," ghostly, and worse, a "Cold Pastoral" that teases us "out of thought," as does "eternity." Eternity, the urn, are sinister. Both suggest a realm of pleasure we desperately desire—a place of no division, pain, death—but can never reach, and so remind us of what we can't have but want, and what we do have—death, pain, strife—but loathe.

The poet is reading intensely now, imagining this vase from one angle after another, each revealing a new virtue or limitation. He shifts again, now viewing the urn once more in a positive light: after all of us have died, the urn will remain, and be a friend to future generations just as woeful as ours, by saying to them—as it says to us—that beauty and truth are the same, and that's all the knowledge we will ever need. How can an urn that makes us crazy with unfulfilled desire one minute comfort us in the next?

The urn reveals the gap between life and art as both lamentable and uplifting: lamentable because it reveals our human limitation, elevating because it alerts us to amplitudes beyond our cognitive habits. The urn as foe and friend: this is clear. But the poem again veers toward ambiguity. The conclusion on truth and beauty has puzzled Keats readers as a koan would a student of Zen. We could interpret it for pages. But their inscrutability is thematically apt: a poem about a deeply mysterious urn, never to be quite understood, ends with an irresolvable conundrum. We find ourselves in the same position as the poet: just as he broods over the urn, we obsess over the poem.

The poem is our urn. The title is "Ode *on* a Grecian Urn," as though the verse is inscribed in the stone. For our interpretations to be productive, we should once more follow the model of the poet—turn the verse perpetually before our eager imaginations.

Chapter 20

✦

Melancholy

Where are we in the valley of soul-making? "Ode to Psyche" proved a primer on how to read the markers in the vale, find the path. "Ode on Indolence" opened onto the valley proper, revealing the vapidity of being an "intelligence," a mere escapist, and demonstrating the abundant possibilities of making an identity. "Ode on a Grecian Urn" pushes far into the gorge, showing an acute understanding of life's sufferings—fevers and thirsts—and wondering how art might salve them. The poem suggests that suffering is a muse of art—it inspires us to create artifices that might transcend the torment—but also a product of art. The poet's pain arouses his desire to escape the pain through his art; but then his art, by reminding him of the inescapability of his pain, only intensifies the suffering.

I am an inveterate escapist, adorer of old Hollywood studio movies, science fiction and crime novels, sleep, gin, Pre-Raphaelite art, NFL football. Anything to dupe me into forgetting, for a moment, my troubles. Some such flights seem necessary for balance, little rests (like those offered by the moony gardens of Blake's Beulah) reviving me for artistic struggle (the mental hunting that Blake describes as Eden). But when the breaks pervert into life's main purpose, then the garden, to continue with Blake, calcifies into hell. Living with your mom and dad for a few months after graduation is a healthy refueling. But to live in your parents' basement deep into your twenties: this is arrested development, time as a prison.

I rush to the cellar, my gloomy man cave, to escape my depression. But the unproductive gloom really deepens the darkness, divorcing me from the chiaroscuro currents, potentially salubrious, of life above ground. I need to climb out of the pen into the rough play of day, where grace happens when the most intense black creates the brightest light. This is the mercy of melancholy, depression's more capacious twin: the converting of death into life, to art.

Keats's "Ode on Melancholy" denounces escapism.

No, no, go not to Lethe, neither twist
   Wolf's-bane, tight-rooted, for its poisonous wine;
Nor suffer thy pale forehead to be kiss'd
   By nightshade, ruby grape of Proserpine;
   Make not your rosary of yew-berries,
   Nor let the beetle, nor the death-moth be
     Your mournful Psyche, nor the downy owl
A partner in your sorrow's mysteries;
   For shade to shade will come too drowsily,
     And drown the wakeful anguish of the soul.

Don't go to drugged-out oblivion, or kill yourself, or tame your melancholy by fitting it into Gothic conventions. Dope and trope alike dull what the poet most wants to feel: melancholy, the "wakeful anguish of the soul."

This anguish readies one for the "melancholy fit," in which our sadness vitalizes our aesthetic sensibilities.

But when the melancholy fit shall fall
   Sudden from heaven like a weeping cloud,
That fosters the droop-headed flowers all,
   And hides the green hill in an April shroud;
Then glut thy sorrow on a morning rose,
   Or on the rainbow of the salt sand-wave,
   Or on the wealth of globed peonies;
Or if thy mistress some rich anger shows,
   Emprison her soft hand, and let her rave,
     And feed deep, deep upon her peerless eyes.

The fit, coming to those who embrace sorrow as a necessary part of life, is duplicitous. Dropping from the bright heavens in a grim mist, nourishing and smothering flowers, the mood marries death and beauty. When jolted by this conjunction, we should "glut"—satiate, gorge—our sorrows on dying natural beauty: roses, rainbows, peonies. Or we can feed our woe with human beauty, "emprison" the hand of a gorgeous, rotting woman, take in her features.

This mistress is most beautiful when most mortal. She, along with the rose, rainbow, and flower,

dwells with Beauty—Beauty that must die;
And Joy, whose hand is ever at his lips

> Bidding adieu; and aching Pleasure nigh,
> Turning to poison while the bee-mouth sips.

Memento mori conjures carpe diem: to dwell deeply on death is to realize one's radical finitude and to intensify the time one has left. Death inspires beauty; beauty fuels death's rush.

A synonymous relationship occurs to the poet: between delight and sorrow.

> Ay, in the very temple of Delight
>   Veil'd Melancholy has her sovran shrine,
>   Though seen of none save him whose strenuous tongue
>   Can burst Joy's grape against his palate fine;
> His soul shalt taste the sadness of her might,
>   And be among her cloudy trophies hung.

When we are happiest over earth's glories, we become most sad, realizing that these greens are going. The sadness generates joy, ecstasy in the current verdure. A ratio arises: the heavier the sorrow, the higher the happiness. The imperative: die hard, live high.

Melancholy is, as was Psyche, divine. Her shrine, lying within temple of Delight, improves on the Psyche fane. Unlike Psyche's fanciful mental temple, Melancholy's is grounded in the actual, where sorrow holds sway, and more attuned to life's painful conflicts. The form of devotion is different, too. The devotee of Psyche fashions interior artifices unifying time and eternity, too good to be true. The worshipper of Melancholy practices rituals too true to be good. He enters into a temple not of his own making: the world into which he, like all of us, was flung at birth, where sadness originates delight. He must conform to the temple's rules for worship. The code most efficacious for an experience of the sacred is to live furiously, die young, become one of the death goddess's "cloudy trophies": stuffed corpses.

The taxidermy lacks focus. Like all trophies, it tries to freeze-frame a winning moment, lift it above deadly time, but the instant is too quick to capture. The memorial is blurred, ambiguous.

What shape does this poet's trophy take? The ode itself, which commemorates his understanding of Melancholy's religion. The ode's cloudiness—its chiaroscuro of moods—reflects life's mistiness. To read well the fog, we must, like the poet, submit to the deadly fumes. Going low, we rise in soul-making's valley.

Chapter 21

✦

Nightingale

"Ode on a Grecian Urn" dramatizes: "I want out of the fight"; "Ode on Melancholy," "I'm ready to mix it up." "Ode to a Nightingale" depicts a more complicated, ambitious mood: when we want the great fullness of life, stillness and motion simultaneously, tranquility and turbulence.

Where "Ode on Melancholy" renounced opiates, "Ode to a Nightingale" shows a poet thoroughly drugged.

> My heart aches, and a drowsy numbness pains
>   My sense, as though of hemlock I had drunk,
> Or emptied some dull opiate to the drains
>   One minute past, and Lethe-wards had sunk:
> 'Tis not through envy of thy happy lot,
>   But being too happy in thine happiness,—
>   That thou, light-winged Dryad of the trees
>   In some melodious plot
>   Of beechen green, and shadows numberless,
>   Singest of summer in full-throated ease.

The poet's emotional pain is so intense he's about to pass out. His mind is going blank, as if poison is killing it or some strong narcotic shutting it down. Is this a figurative description of torment, or does it betray a suicidal wish? The poet definitely wants to escape his ache. Self-slaughter is an option.

His escapist fantasies center on the nightingale. He shifts from his pain to claiming that he's not envious of the bird for possessing a happiness he lacks, but rather is "too happy" in the bird's pleasure. That he says he's not envious implies that he's actually felt envious, and perhaps still does. Envy would be understandable, given that the bird seems to enjoy precisely the bliss he lacks. While he is sinking into miserable, mute stupor, the lightsome bird effortlessly sings of the most vital season.

But let's assume that the poet really is "too happy" in the bird's happiness. How can he, so despairing, claim he's happy at all? Surely he means this happiness in a hypothetical way, essentially saying: "I can imagine what happiness is like, even if I don't now feel happy; happiness is like what you are experiencing, bird, right now."

The poet's feelings are mixed: envy toward a creature enjoying what he can't; desire for qualities he can never possess; admiration of these qualities. But these traits might not actually belong to the bird at all. The poet might well just be praising an imaginative projection. The nightingale is a "Dryad," a mythological being, and it sings in "shadows numberless," suggesting that it's a shade beyond quantification.

In the next stanza, the poet wonders if his imagination might liberate him from torment. It can translate a tweeting thing into a deathless Dryad. Why not create more ravishing fantasies?

> O, for a draught of vintage! that hath been
>   Cool'd a long age in the deep-delved earth,
>   Tasting of Flora and the country green,
> Dance, and Provençal song, and sunburnt mirth!
> O for a beaker full of the warm South,
>   Full of the true, the blushful Hippocrene,
>   With beaded bubbles winking at the brim,
>   And purple-stained mouth;
>   That I might drink, and leave the world unseen,
>   And with thee fade away into the forest dim:

The world is purely mythological. The goddess of flowers might appear, as might the spring sacred to the Muses. The wine for which the poet longs contains this stream, true poetic inspiration. To drink this wine is to fade away from this tortured world and find oneself at one with the bird, now clearly supernatural, the miraculous result of a magical beverage.

The poet in the next stanza struggles to free himself from agonies that this unreal bird has never known: "The weariness, the fever, and the fret / Here, where men sit and hear each other groan." But he can't escape. His fantasy of a mythological paradise and its magical wine didn't carry him far enough. And so he leaps out of the chariot of "Bacchus and his pards" and claims, in the subsequent stanza, a new vehicle for his emancipation: the "viewless wings of Poesy."

Even though he's getting tired—his "dull brain perplexes and retards"—he mounts Poesy and catches up with the bird. "Already with thee!" he cheers. The two of them rise to the heavens, where, by good fortune, the "Queen-Moon is on her throne, / Cluster'd around by all her starry Fays." The poet can't maintain the imaginative vitality, however. All goes dark: "here there is no light, / Save what from heaven is with the breezes blown / Through verdurous glooms and winding mossy ways."

The poet has retreated too far into his mental world, divorcing himself from the vivid sights of the physical. The "viewless" wings of poetry might be invisible, spiritual, untroubled by space and time, but they are also blind, unable to view: too fixed on the shadows of the imagination to perceive actual light.

Here we come to the poet's terrible bind. He wants to free himself from the pain of time. But whenever he imagines the unearthly paradise, he envisions rapturously sensual experiences. He loves the temporal in spite of himself.

Deep in the recesses of his own dark head, he realizes this affection, and laments his cognitive distance from earth.

> I cannot see what flowers are at my feet,
>   Nor what soft incense hangs upon the boughs,
> But, in embalmed darkness, guess each sweet
>   Wherewith the seasonable month endows
> The grass, the thicket, and the fruit-tree wild;
>   White hawthorn, and the pastoral eglantine;
>   Fast fading violets cover'd up in leaves;
>   And mid-May's eldest child,
>   The coming musk-rose, full of dewy wine,
>   The murmurous haunt of flies on summer eves.

Keats returns to the equation in *The Eve of St. Agnes*: escapism, literary or otherwise, is suicide. In this case, the poet regrets his effort to flee time, though he has in the past frequently been "half in love with easeful Death"—as he confesses in the next stanza. He would actually consider self-slaughter again, but he realizes that if he did, he would never again hear the bird's gorgeous song, just now pouring ecstatically forth. To the nightingale's "high requiem," he would "become a sod."

The poet aspires to the ideal, and he distances earth's beauty. He dives into the actual, he suffers loss and pain. How can he move out of this paralysis?

He does what Keats has so often done, in person and in his poetic personae: he rouses himself from his narcissism, flings his imagination out of his own interiors, and empathizes with the mysterious vitalities of another. He turns again, in the penultimate stanza, to the bird: "Thou wast not born for death, immortal Bird / No hungry generations tread thee down." Its song was heard in "ancient days by emperor and clown," and perhaps "found a path / Through the sad heart of Ruth, when, sick for home, / She stood in tears amid the alien corn."

How is this attribution of limitlessness to an obviously mortal animal any different from the poet using the bird as an occasion for an escapist fantasy? The bird in this context is not supernatural but simply an animal that lacks an awareness of, and thus fear of, death. The bird wasn't born for death because it has no conception of death. It simply *is*, unhindered and unhurt by the terrible gap that enervates the poet, between what must be endured and what is desired. Identifying with this characteristic of the bird, the poet senses what it would be like to be untroubled by time, not hollowed by nostalgia or regret, anticipation or dread, but in the moment, the pure present. Exhilarated, he frees himself from history, *becomes*, imaginatively, ancient emperor and biblical Ruth.

He can't hold timelessness for long, contentment with the actual. Feeling the pain of Ruth, he flees again to fantasy. He pictures the bird singing near "magic casements" that open on the "foam of perilous seas" in "faery lands forlorn."

This time, though, he doesn't languish in folklore. No longer numb or drowsy, his mind is now agile, alert, attuned to what is. He is not a bird tweeting near magical oceans; he is a man struggling with despair. It is he, and not the fairy, who is "forlorn."

> Forlorn! the very word is like a bell
>   To toll me back from thee to my sole self!
> Adieu! the fancy cannot cheat so well
>   As she is fam'd to do, deceiving elf.
> Adieu! adieu! thy plaintive anthem fades
>   Past the near meadows, over the still stream,
>   Up the hill-side; and now 'tis buried deep
>   In the next valley-glades:
> Was it a vision, or a waking dream?
> Fled is that music:—Do I wake or sleep?

This abrupt return to his sorrowful subjectivity in the final stanza seems like a defeat: a man who tried to overcome his suicidal depression with his imagination has failed, and has fallen right back to the painful state from which he began.

But this poet clearly has a different understanding of his life than he did at the beginning of his meditation. Note that the word "forlorn" summons him back to his depression like a bell. A tolling bell suggests the funeral clanging Donne so powerfully evoked, and so tells us that the poet has returned to his death obsession. A bell, though, is also celebratory; we don't need Tennyson's "Ring Out, Wild Bells" to tell us that. The poet's "sole self" isn't simply woeful and lonely; it is also newly vitalized, resurrected: by way of a pun, a "soul" self.

The poet's mind is quite animated at this point, rapidly vacillating among ideas and moods. "Adieu!" he exclaims to the vanishing bird, with no lamentation in his tone. No need to be sad just now; he is brimming with insight. His "fancy," he realizes, is prone to cheat, to deceive him into believing in magical brews and moon queens that don't exist. But there's no reason to scold this deceptive part of his mind; rather, just poke a bit of fun, call it an elf on the con. Indeed, the imagination, despite its cunning, is as close to magic as one can come in this material world. It is an elf that deceives, but also a sprite, a spirit, and so not bound by physics, and capable of conjuring something from nothing, transforming one thing into another, despair into hope.

The poet no longer feels trapped between two equally tragic poles: either latch onto the ideal and lose earth's beauty, or hold to the actual and find no respite from death. Now he senses each antinomy's virtues as well as its limitations, and enjoys freely flitting back and forth, finding fresh energy with each turn. The ideal realm, though bloodless, can transform horror into beauty; and the actual, although bloody as hell, can invigorate the heart.

This balancing act continues. Goodbye again, the poet says to the bird, whose "plaintive anthem" dissolves into the distance, a reason for sorrow, since the song has been so beautiful, but a reason for happiness as well, because the poet's interactions with the nightingale have revived him. Picturing the bird's leaving, he emphasizes the positive, alive to its actual motions, its graceful gliding over a meadow, a tranquil stream, a hillside, a deep valley.

Having bid bittersweet farewell to the creature, the poet shifts again to himself. He asks, as one would after undergoing such a compelling encounter: what really just happened? Did I have these experiences? Or did I dream them? Should I take these insights on ideal and actual seriously? Or were they just wispy fragments of a hypnogogic reverie? It appears that he can't answer. How could he? Does he care? Does he descend into debilitating navel-gazing? No. He simply announces what he does know: the music is gone. Then he reveals what he doesn't know: whether he is awake or asleep.

So the poem concludes in uncertainty, but unsureness to which the poet is reconciled. He has reached negative capability at its most exquisite, that rare moment when one hovers alertly, charged with anticipation, among numerous possibilities. Keats intimated such a state in "Ode on Indolence," which ends with the poet suspended in acute curiosity. Achieving such a condition in that poem was rather easy, a slight elevation from lazy indifference. Here, in "Ode to a Nightingale," reaching this wise passivity—Wordsworth's phrase—is severely difficult, since the poet begins in a suicidal depression. Perhaps because it emerges from despair, this instance of negative capability is richer, more varied, compelling, potent, on the verge of major insights on art and life, dreaming and wakefulness, madness and sanity.

These moments are blue-moon rare, and the poem shows why: the balance is extremely precarious. The ode closes with the poet quivering in doubt—which he appears to accept, but doubt nonetheless, that can quickly turn into frustration: negative *in*capability.

At poem's end, we find ourselves, as we have with the other odes, in the same position as the poet: balanced, just barely, between clarity and confusion. What to do? Return to the dreaminess at the start, follow the poet through the maze once more, hoping the confusion will become more lucid, and the lucidity, fruitfully muddled.

Chapter 22

✦

Autumn

How inspiriting to reach for unattainable beauties—shaded nightingales, odes about nightingales, Xanadus, Byzantiums, Edens, Daisy Buchanans; and how, as Jay Gatsby excruciatingly knew, agonizing. To encompass both pain and ecstasy in one vision—this feels like a kind of wisdom, of the sort the "myriad-minded" (Coleridge's term) Shakespeare possessed. But what if one could gain utmost joy not in reconciling life's antagonisms between what is and what ought to be, the true and the beautiful, but rather in doing away with the rift entirely, simply accepting existence right here, right now, as perfectly adequate: a bird skeleton discovered with your daughter, your daughter looking for the first time at the bones, the scattered feathers, the coming winter sky in which this bird will never fly?

To find abundant delight in the ordinary, the everyday: this seems easy and impossible at once. Here's your child. Love her and be content. Here's your child: lovely as she is, she could be better.

For me, besotted with precious art and depressively disdainful toward the quotidian, love of the "is" has been elusive, while yearning for the "ought" has proved sovereign. The result: enjoying neither what actually exists (nothing is good enough), nor could exist (the good is ghostly).

Like a cross to a Christian, or to a Buddhist a mandala, Keats's "To Autumn" is to me an emblem for utter reconciliation—between the permanent and the passing, the sacred and the profane, unity and diversity. I return to this fictional perfection constantly, a fantasy—such unperturbedness could never exist in this turbid world—that nonetheless assuages the facts. Even if I can never achieve the tranquility, my meditations on it at least slow my conflicts, as would an imagined light that somehow makes the dark seem less black.

In June of his brilliant summer of 1819, Keats moved to Shanklin, on the Isle of Wight, in order to save money on rent and to find the peace (really some distance from the all-consuming Fanny) to develop marketable literary projects: *Otho the Great*, a drama, and *Lamia*, a romance. By early August, he and Brown had gotten as far as they could on the play without further research on their protagonist, a Roman emperor. And so they moved to Winchester, to use the town's library. On September 21, in a letter to Reynolds, Keats praised the autumnal landscape surrounding the village: "How beautiful the season is now—How fine the air. A temperate sharpness about it. Really, without joking, chaste weather—Dian skies—I never lik'd stubble fields so much as now—Aye better than the chilly green of spring. Somehow a stubble plain looks warm—in the same way that some pictures look warm—this struck me so much in my Sunday's walk that I composed upon it."

This composition was "To Autumn," completed on September 19. To call the poem "perfect" is by now a tedious critical commonplace, but the adjective does point to the poem's most salient qualities: its graceful three-part structure, moving gently from luminous early fall to pre-winter twilight; its harmonious blending of growth and decay; the aptness of its imagery, visually sumptuous at the beginning, in the end more focused on plaintive sounds; and its calmness of tone, bespeaking a tender embrace of what is, as though all is as it should be, with no drama, no struggle. Indeed, the poet doesn't even show up as character: no "I" explores his sorrows and joys. The poet stands to the side, and points with his words to the beauty of the season, when time's waves have calmed to effortless ripples, so regular in their bright rises and dives that they seem not to move.

When such a perfect instant comes, is it the result of certain behaviors, the peak of a difficult climb, or is it accidental, a lucky break? The answer to this inquiry requires the answer to another question: what is grace? "To Autumn" tells us.

> Season of mists and mellow fruitfulness,
>   Close bosom-friend of the maturing sun;
> Conspiring with him how to load and bless
>   With fruit the vines that round the thatch-eves run;
> To bend with apples the moss'd cottage-trees,
>   And fill all fruit with ripeness to the core;
>   To swell the gourd, and plump the hazel shells
>   With a sweet kernel; to set budding more,
> And still more, later flowers for the bees,
> Until they think warm days will never cease,
>   For summer has o'er-brimm'd their clammy cells.

The distinction between mist and growth has faded: nurturing the growth to its height, the mist is the ripeness; manifesting the nourishment of the mist, the fruitfulness is the cloud. These autumnal elements welcome a third—the sun. As with mists and fruitfulness, so the action of the sun—itself indistinct from the mist its vehicle and the fruitfulness its result—becomes one with the produce it nurtures. The expansions and swellings and gains: these are what the sun does—it's not the sun without doing so—just as the sun's energy is what the growths are—they are not beings without the beams. Mist, fruitfulness, sun, growth: these energies create patterns that are themselves intertwined so intimately that discrete strands disappear into the whole. The vines become the thatch; moss and bark merge; flower sustains bee, bee pollinates flower; summer and autumn are indistinct.

The frequent use of the infinitive connects these autumnal activities to more general seasonal rhythms. An infinitive is a verb not yet tensed into past, present, or future, not put into variegated play; but the infinitive does express action—marks movement, causality, change. It is thus a grammatical marriage of being and becoming, unity and multiplicity. "To load," "to bless," "to bend," "to fill," "to swell," "to plumb," "to set": these are the serene vehicles of this autumn's unmoving motions. Existence, the poem intimates, is like this all the time: still within the flux. Why do we so rarely experience the world this way? The poet implies this question at the beginning of the next stanza. In his first appearance in the verse—not as an empathetic "I" but as an unobtrusive inquirer—he asks: "Who hath not seen thee oft amid thy store?" The question is rhetorical, assertion and conjecture, meaning: "It would seem that everyone has seen you, Autumn, in the midst of your produce." A question that is and is not, a claim that exists but doesn't: these are ironic situations, and reinforce the persistent irony of the first stanza, which describes actions that aren't actions, differences that aren't differences.

The stanza's next line continues the irony. After basically saying, "Everyone has seen fall amidst its products," the poet reverses, suggesting that people only occasionally perceive autumn: "Sometimes whoever seeks abroad may find / Thee . . . ." The contradiction in paraphrase: "Everyone has probably seen you abroad; only sometimes, if someone is actually seeking you, he'll see you." This seems to mean: "Everyone could see you—that is—perceive your gentle synthesis—if he wanted, but actually not everyone does." So, who does? The poet answers, by personifying autumn in a very particular fashion.

Sometimes whoever seeks abroad may find
Thee sitting careless on a granary floor,
    Thy hair soft-lifted by the winnowing wind;
Or on a half-reap'd furrow sound asleep,
    Drows'd with the fume of poppies, while thy hook
        Spares the next swath and all its twined flowers:
And sometimes like a gleaner thou dost keep
    Steady thy laden head across a brook;
    Or by a cyder-press, with patient look,
        Thou watchest the last oozings hours by hours.

There is more than one way to personify. One can turn the land into a reflection of his ego. Ahab does this when he translates the White Whale into a symbol of all of the evils he himself has endured. This kind of personification is "selfing." Another sort is "othering"—the effort to "live into" the land, to perceive as it might perceive. In attempting to experience the world as a whale might, Melville's Ishmael practices this mode, sensitive to how nature actually functions.

Keats's poet "others" in "To Autumn." He inhabits the season. Aware of autumn's marriage of stillness and motion, he imagines the season lounging carelessly among the grains, with her hair floating freely, as does the grain, in the winnowing wind. Or she reclines drowsily on a furrow half-harvested, her scythe resting beside her. But the poet is also sensitive in this second stanza to labor, autumn not at rest. It is harvest time, and the effortless growths of the first stanza must now be gathered and stored. The labor is not difficult, however. Autumn as gleaner is steady; as maker of cider, she is patient. The work, though necessary, is rewarding, generating beauty and bounty.

The human labor, though it requires will and energy, occurs as naturally and as effortlessly as nuts plumping. Note the imagery: autumn as a gleaner arches across a brook, suggesting that she unifies oppositions—one bank and another—and is part of a larger flow. As a presser of cider, she calmly studies how destruction—of apples—is actually creative—of a nourishing drink—and how, analogously, the dissolution of matter to muck is an integral part of the grand harmony.

The poet's personifying is his way of participating in the season's work. Just as the sun ripens, the poet empathetically depicts the fall's beauties. He removes himself from his description as much as possible, making sure that his ego doesn't cloud the view. He is in the poem and out of it, there and not, active and passive, creator and conduit. This ironic disposition, acting through non-acting, becoming as the infinitive, seems necessary for properly seeking autumn abroad.

The ode has moved from early autumn, almost inseparable from summer, to the middle, when harvesters gather the produce. Describing this progression, the poet has gained a more intimate understanding of the season. In the first stanza, he stood to the side. In the second, he injected himself into the landscape. Now, in the third, as the season verges on winter, he continues to personify the season, but now as a conversational companion, a close friend. Speaking directly to her, he demonstrates his knowledge of her secrets and reminds her of her glory. "Where are the songs of spring? Ay, where are they? / Think not of them, thou has thy music, too."

> While barred clouds bloom the soft-dying day,
>   And touch the stubble-plains with rosy hue;
> Then in a wailful choir the small gnats mourn
>   Among the river sallows, borne aloft
>   Or sinking as the light wind lives or dies;
> And full-grown lambs loud bleat from hilly bourn;
>   Hedge-crickets sing; and now with treble soft
> The red-breast whistles from a garden-croft;
>   And gathering swallows twitter in the skies.

The winter darkness encroaches. The colors of ripening and harvest fade. Only plaintive sounds are heard. Gnats, wavering in the light wind, mourn; lambs old enough to be slaughtered bleat from the hills; crickets sing; robins whistle; and swallows twitter as they prepare for their migration.

"Darkling" the poet "listens," and indeed is half in love with "easeful death," but now there is no psychological torment that he might briefly calm by balancing the combatants, and now there is no suicidal wishing. The listening in the dark is listening in the dark, and loving the longing sounds in light just gone. And the impending death, inevitable as winter, is easeful because it is part of an expansive cycle that is, even in decay, exquisite. The poet, staring (and listening) with astonishment, has realized what Keats knew the greatest poets, like Shakespeare, knew: that when the artist beholds what is, and doesn't pass judgment but rather says "yes" to, "blesses" the moment, in all of its mysteriousness, he finds it beautiful.

Can we foster these moments, when all gently consent? Yes, Keats would say, if we see the world as a vale of soul-making, and thus its pains and mysteries as necessary for revealing to us who we are, and what we can do.

But these moments of rightness, when all is forgiven, and grace abounds, are fleeting. They are already twittering away into the darkening skies. So "To Autumn" trails off, with the birds gathering to abandon the chilly land. They will soon be gone, and the poet will find himself darkling in painful earnest, bereft, with aching heart and fantasies of flying. He will then revert to those torments of the earlier odes, the weariness and the fret, the groaning and dying, the parching tongue, the exhausting doubts over what's feigned and what's real. He will live through all of the odes again, as he will live through all the moods and all the seasons, but with each return, if he remains committed to making his soul, he will know more, be more alive, truer in his beauties.

Chapter 23

✦

A Tear Is an Intellectual Thing

On the track of beauties that have so eluded me, I traveled to Rome in the early summer of 2012, for Caravaggio—his luminous grimness—and for Keats. Having begun my sojourn overseas in London, Keats's birthplace, I thought fit to end it—I would return to America in early June—in the city where Keats died.

On the afternoon of the morning I toured the Borghese, I visited the Keats-Shelley House, located just to the right of the Spanish Steps, if you're facing them. I quickly walked through the outer rooms of the house. I wanted to reach where something tremendous had happened: the death of the writer I loved most.

I was surprised at the smallness of the room, and imagined how the poet who rose to Staffa's god-colossal basalt felt in such a confined space. At first he probably hated the closeness, re-breathing the sick air that had no place to go. Over the weeks, though, as he retreated deeper into his sickness, he probably grew indifferent to any surroundings, near or far. Cursed by his empathy, he became his rotting lungs.

In the room, there is a replica of Keats's bed. (The original one was burned, like everything else in the house, by the Roman authorities, who feared contagion.) Near the bed hangs Severn's drawing of Keats, executed only days from the death. The poet is haggard, emaciated, with fever-sweat matting his hair to his forehead. He doesn't look peaceful. He is weak, resigned.

I was in the room alone, Sandi and Una having stopped in the gift shop on the way in. I had come here for the same reason I had earlier visited other Keats landmarks: to have an *experience*, a more intense intimacy with the poet.

The inconsequential particular torques the heart. For no good reason, I glanced at the floor at the base of the bed, noticed a patch of dust, and into my mind slammed: an image of Keats's blood-spit splattering this floor.

That was one of the agonies of his consumption, lung hemorrhaging so profuse that his own blood choked him. He must have hocked it up by the pint. Severn couldn't have always been right there with the bucket. Keats stained his last life on the marble.

The magnitude of Keats's art contrasted with the ignominy of sputum: this is what I initially felt, but then pulled back, thinking, how obvious, how trite, a conceit that might organize a sophomoric poem.

The caring over trifles collapsed, and hotness from inside my skull pressed against my eyeballs: the burn of coming tears, eclipse-sparse in my life, which has been a long defense against the vulnerability of real feeling, borne of a fear that raw emotion would be my dark undoing. I cried, not conspicuously, but silently, two small streams leaking from my eyes.

The crying wasn't simple sadness, was by no means joy; more like, a feeling too immense and forceful and confused for my frame to hold. Keats, exuberant poet and robust romancer, bereft of verse and love; pugnaciously confident, now dwindled to bleeding, spitting, vomiting, shitting; large noble soul, generous and funny, reduced to suicidal desperation, violent anger: the tragedy of these facts agitated one layer of feeling.

Another layer was more self-absorbed: Keats no longer exists, and I need him to, to write about what it's like to be forty-five, with wife and child, still with aspirations to compose powerfully, and with numbing depression.

Still other layers, even closer to my bones: I will never approach Keats's talent; at this potentially sublime moment in Rome, I emit only clichés; I lack Keats's empathy; I am unworthy to write about him; my suffering, compared to his, is minimal, yet I constantly complain.

Within the perplexity, though, was rapture. Keats *existed*, and wrote what he did, and that, in this brute, stupid world, is miraculous. I can read his Odes whenever I want. I understand them well enough. I am here right now, in the Eternal City, at this literary landmark. I have a sweet child and wife who love me, whom I love. I have written decent books and am capable of writing more.

And finally, the more general bewildering bliss of vague universals: life is so sad we should end it now; life is so sweet let's hold to it hard; death brings clarity; dying is meaningless; look at the greatness of suffering honestly embraced; hurting is hurting is hurting; I can't *believe* this is happening, since existence is so wasteful, poets full of promise succumbing young; and I can't believe *this* is happening, life is so mysteriously superabundant.

All of this, and more I couldn't and can't articulate, overwhelmed me, pressed for expression more visceral than words: tears.

Blake once wrote, "a Tear is an Intellectual Thing."[1] He meant that in a world frequently merciless and cruel, strong sorrowful emotion reveals a sensitive understanding of the world's suffering, a thoughtful, empathetic challenge to the prideful rigidity of the tyrant.

Why did I wipe my eyes as Sandi and Una approached, and turn my head from them when they arrived in the room? The same question more troublingly applies to a scene from the next day, during which we visited the Protestant Cemetery, also in Rome, where Keats is buried. At the grave, I explained to Una how Sandi and I had visited this site together over twenty years ago, on a college trip. Una then said that we each should read a Keats poem, to pay our respects to this memory and to the poet. At my suggestion, she read "When I Have Fears." Sandi, also taking my cue, read "Why Did I Laugh Tonight?" That left for me, the third of the death sonnets, "Bright Star." I began to recite the verses. I sensed the same pressing that brought tears the day before. I swallowed hard, clenched my jaw, and thought, while saying "still steadfast, still unchangeable": "I will not cry."

If Blake is right about tears, holding them back is brutish, shutting down authentic sadness and the empathy that attends. In the chamber where Keats died, my ego fell aside, and feeling from being to being flowed. But so soon the "I saying I," clogged again the works.

The door to the third room had opened. Halfway into the mist, I had faltered, turned back, slammed the door behind me, retreated into the corridors through which I had emerged, and stood resolute in my fear. Is the door still where it was?

Chapter 24

✦

I Shall Die Easy

Almost immediately after Keats completed "To Autumn," he stumbled into darkness far blacker than the third room's gloom. The brutal realities he had been battling for the past three years overwhelmed him. The poem's equilibrium eluded him, and, worse, so, for the most part, did his muse. He wrote very little after watching the night engulf the swallows, and nothing that matched, in depth, insight, and musicality, the odes.

Keats's sore throat finally revealed its true and sinister nature on February 3, 1820. He had spent the cold evening riding through London on the top of a coach, too poor to pay for the cab. When he reached Wentworth, to which he had returned from Winchester in late October, he appeared before Brown haggard, flushed, fevered. Upon his friend's advice, Keats went to bed immediately. Before he could find rest, though, he suffered a severe hemorrhage of the lungs and coughed up blood. Once he recovered, he asked Brown for a candle. Keats held the flame close to a blood-stain on the sheet, and said: "I know the colour of that blood;—it is arterial blood;—I cannot be deceived in that colour;—that drop of blood is my death-warrant;—I must die."

That Keats chose to chill his already ailing body in the damp winter air is shocking, until we remember that he was severely troubled, and possibly suicidal, over an incident that had occurred only a few days earlier. He had met his brother George, recently returned from America, where he had migrated soon after his marriage to seek his fortune. George's venture, based in Kentucky (he is actually buried there), was not thriving, and he was in terrible need of funds. He sailed home to ask his brother for help. For perhaps the first time ever, Keats quarreled with his brother over the inheritance. In the end, John gave George £700, leaving himself with only about £60 or £70. This reduced Keats to poverty, and the argument alienated him from his brother to the point that George didn't even say goodbye to John when he sailed back to America on January 28. From this point on, Keats was basically dependent upon his friends' charity, and increasingly, and bitterly, certain that he would never raise enough money to marry Fanny, even if he could live long enough to do it.

Most of the remaining year of his life—he would die on February 23 of 1821—he was consumed with Fanny, persistently vowing his desperate love for her in letter after letter. This epistle from March 1820 is typical:

> You fear, sometimes, I do not love you so much as you wish? My dear Girl I love you ever and ever and without reserve. The more I have known you the more have I lov'd. In every way—even my jealousies have been agonies of Love, in the hottest fit I ever had I would have died for you. I have vex'd you too much. But for Love! Can I help it? You are always new. The last of your kisses was ever the sweetest; the last smile the brightest; the last movement the gracefullest. When you pass'd my window home yesterday, I was fill'd with as much admiration as if I had then seen you for the first time. You uttered a half complaint once that I only lov'd your Beauty. Have I nothing else then to love in you but that. Do not I see a heart naturally furnish'd with wings imprison itself with me? No ill prospect has been able to turn your thoughts a moment from me. This perhaps should be as much a subject of sorrow as joy—but I will not talk of that. Even if you did not love me I could not help an entire devotion to you: how much more deeply then must I feel for you knowing you love me. My Mind has been the most discontented and restless one that ever was put into a body too small for it. I never felt my Mind repose upon anything with complete and undistracted enjoyment—upon no person but you. When you are in the room my thoughts never fly out of window: you always concentrate my whole senses. The anxiety shown about our Love in your last note is an immense pleasure to me; however you must not suffer such speculations to molest you any more: not will I any more believe you can have the least pique against me.

Keats wrote many such emotionally vulnerable letters to Fanny. Some of them were not this sweet, but jealous, petulant, abject, and selfish. When the frenzied letters became public many years after Keats's death, they disappointed many of his admirers.

These epistles are far from exemplary. Why should they be, we in our more confessional age would ask? This was a man sick with love, but too ill in body ever to enjoy consummation's healing. His vision of the necessity of suffering for the making of a soul could not restore his heart.

When Keats understood, after several weeks in Rome, that he would probably never see Fanny again, he was almost disgusted by his former wisdom, finding it nothing but a reminder of what he now lacked. Here he is in his final known letter, addressed to Brown: "There is one thought enough to kill me—I have been well, healthy, alert & c, walking with her—and now—the knowledge of contrast, feeling for light and shade, all that information (primitive sense) necessary for a poem are great enemies to the recovery of my stomach." Poetry now lost to him, and his life's love, too, he couldn't stand being reminded of either. He refused to open the letters Fanny sent to him once he reached Rome, simply incapable of entertaining the future ripped from him. He was buried with her unread words.

At least Keats did get to see the publication of his final book. In July 1820, Taylor and Hessey released *Lamia, Isabella, The Eve of St. Agnes, and Other Poems.* The volume, which included five of the odes, was well received. No one had an inkling, though, of the genius of these poems, or of how famous they would become. And so Keats sailed to Rome in September with the moderate satisfaction of getting some good reviews, but with no way of knowing that he would one day really be among the English poets. As far as he knew, he was destined for oblivion.

In his final days in Rome, Keats's depression and illness reduced him to little more than a body starving for relief. All of Keats's energies were focused on how to escape the pain even for a minute—Severn's playing of music sometimes helped—or on his anger over his cruel plight. He pitched fits, screaming at Severn, accusing his friend of poisoning him. He threw his unwanted meals at his well-meaning companion, or out the window into the street below. He tried to kill himself with laudanum, and howled when Severn restrained him.

Keats's imagination, his soul-making, had shut down. What man in this situation could maintain intellectual elasticity required for negative capability, egolessness, the delighted stare, the eye's leap, the ability to read the mysteries of the heart? Keats's decline in spirit from the day of his first hemorrhage, his abandonment of poetry and love, his jealous outbursts and unseemly fits and suicide attempt: these remind us that Keats was in the end what he was throughout, a bare, forked animal like the rest of us, though a creature endowed with more generosity, geniality, courage, and imagination than most.

The final time we watch the poet, in Severn's last description of him living, these fine traits are on display one last time, in a fitting and graceful exit in which this man laid so low rises once more to an exquisitely soulful gesture, a last moment of empathy, setting his own pain aside to imagine what it's like to be Severn, an exhausted friend and nurse watching his companion and patient die. In his last hours, he looked up, and said, "Severn—I—lift me up—I am dying—I shall die easy—don't be frightened—be firm, and thank God it has come." It did come gently. The bloody phlegm stopped scalding his throat, and his shivering ceased, and death shrouded him like mist descending on fruit.

NOTES

Note to the Reader
1. Walt Whitman, *Song of Myself*, 1.663, in *Leaves of Grass*: The First (1855) Edition, ed. Malcolm Cowley (New York: Penguin, 1961).

2. I don't pretend that this book is an original biography. In fact, I add nothing new to our knowledge of Keats's life. That terrain has been covered thoroughly, and sometimes beautifully, by several distinguished biographers from whose work I have drawn liberally. Foremost, I have drawn from W. Jackson Bates's magisterial *John Keats* (Cambridge, Mass.: Belknap Press of Harvard University Press, 1963); and Stanley Plumly's equally brilliant *Posthumous Keats: A Personal Biography* (New York: Norton, 2009). Nicholas Roe's *John Keats: A New Life* (New Haven, Conn.: Yale University Press, 2013), Denise Gigante's *The Keats Brothers: The Life of George and John* (Cambridge, Mass.: Harvard University Press, 2011), Andrew Motion's *Keats* (London: Faber and Faber, 1998), Robert Gittings's *John Keats* (New York: Little, Brown, 1968), and Aileen Ward's *John Keats: The Making of a Poet* (New York: Viking, 1963) have also been indispensable.

3. In my interpretations of Keats's individual poems, I have been guided by several excellent works of criticism: Dan Beachy-Quick's *Brighter Words Than Bright: Keats at Work* (Iowa City: Iowa University Press, 2013): Shahidha Kazi Bari's *Keats and Philosophy: The Life of Sensations* (New York: Routledge, 2012); Jack Stillinger's *Romantic Complexity: Keats, Coleridge, and Wordsworth* (Urbana: University of Illinois Press, 2008); Mark Sandy's *Poetics of Self and Form in Keats and Shelley: Nietzschean Subjectivity and Genre* (Surrey, Eng.: Ashgate, 2005); Thomas McFarland's *The Mask of Keats: The Endeavor of a Poet* (Oxford: Oxford University Press, 2000); Tom Clark's *Junkets on a Sad Planet: Scenes from the Life of John Keats* (Santa Rosa, Calif.: Black Sparrow, 1994); Stuart M. Sperry's *Keats the Poet* (Princeton, N.J.: Princeton University Press, 1993); Hermione Di Almeida's *Romantic Medicine and John Keats* (New York: Oxford University Press, 1991); Anne K. Mellor's *English Romantic Irony* (Cambridge, Mass.: Harvard University Press, 1980); Helen Vendler's *The Odes of John Keats* (Cambridge, Mass.: Belknap Press of Harvard University Press, 1983); Ronald A. Sharp's *Keats, Skepticism, and the Religion of Beauty* (Athens: University of Georgia Press, 1979); Thomas Weiskel's *The Romantic Sublime: Studies in the Structure and Psychology of Transcendence* (Baltimore: Johns Hopkins University Press, 1976); Morris Dickstein's *Keats and His Poetry: A Study in Development* (Chicago: University of Chicago Press, 1971); Douglas Bush's *John Keats: His Life and Writings* (New York: Macmillan, 1966); Douglas Bush, "Introduction," *Selected Poems and Letters*, by John Keats, ed. Douglas Bush (Boston: Houghton Mifflin, 1959), xi–xvii; Lionel Trilling's "The Poet as Hero: Keats in His Letters," in *The Opposing Self* (New York: Viking, 1955), 3–43; and Robert Gittings's *Keats: The Living Year* (London: Heinemann, 1954).

Chapter 1

1. All quotations from Keats's letters are from *The Letters of John Keats, 1814–1821*, 2 vols., ed. Hyder Edward Rollins (Cambridge, Mass.: Harvard University Press, 1958).

2. Charles Clarke and Mary Cowden Clarke, *Recollections of Writers* (New York: Scribners, 1878), 126.

3. *The Keats Circle: Letters and Papers, 1816–1878*, ed. Hyder Edward Rollins (Cambridge, Mass.: Harvard University Press, 1948), 1:59.

4. Herman Melville, *Moby-Dick; or, The Whale*, ed. Hershel Parker and Harrison Hayford, 2nd ed. (New York: Norton, 1999), 263.

5. F. Scott Fitzgerald, *The Crack-Up*, ed. Edmund Wilson (New York: New Directions, 2009), 57.

6. Wallace Stevens, *The Necessary Angel: Essays on Reality and the Imagination* (New York: Vintage, 1965), 24.

7. Robert D. Richardson, *William James: In the Maelstrom of American Modernism* (Boston: Houghton Mifflin Harcourt, 2006), 492.

Chapter 2

1. Robert Benjamin Haydon, *Life of Robert Benjamin Haydon: Historical Painter, from His Autobiography and Journals*, 2nd ed., ed. Tom Taylor, 3 vols. (London: Longman, Brown, Green, and Longmans, 1853), 1:361.

2. This description from Keats's schoolmate Edward Holmes can be found in Bates, *John Keats*, 21.

3. Clarke, *Recollections of Writers*, 125.

4. I found this striking scene in Bates, *John Keats*, 48.

5. This description of Lucas, from his colleague Astley Cooper, can be found in Motion, *Keats*, 93.

6. Motion highlights these remarks from Clarke and George, 94.

7. Gittings, *John Keats*, 86.

8. Fitzgerald, *The Crack-Up*, 69.

9. This description from Holmes is in *Keats Circle*, 2:164–65.

10. Clarke, *Recollections of Writers*, 130.

11. All quotations of Keats's poetry are from *The Poems of John Keats*, ed. Jack Stillinger (Cambridge, Mass.: Belknap Press of Harvard University Press, 1978).

12. Clarke, *Recollections of Writers*, 133.

13. Leigh Hunt, *Byron and Some of His Contemporaries; with Recollections of the Author's Life and of His Visit to Italy* (Philadelphia: Carey, Lea, and Carey, 1828), 214.

Chapter 3

1. Bates cites this remark from Wordsworth in a January 20, 1817 letter to Haydon, in *John Keats*, 97.

2. Bates cites the harsh letter Ollier wrote in response to George, *John Keats*, 151.

3. C. S. Lewis, *The Pilgrim's Regress*, reprint ed., ill. Michael Hague (Grand Rapids, Mich.: William B. Eerdman, 1992), 204.

4. Herman Melville, "Hawthorne and His Mosses," in Herman Melville, *Moby-Dick; or, The Whale*, ed. Hershel Parker and Harrison Hayford, 2nd ed. (New York: Norton, 1999), 526.

5. Melville, *Moby-Dick*, 59.
6. Melville, *Moby-Dick*, 218.

Chapter 4

1. John Milton, *Paradise Lost*, ed. Stephen Orgel and Jonathan Goldberg, reissue ed. (New York: Oxford University Press, 2008), 5.
2. Milton, *Paradise Lost*, 11.
3. Milton, *Paradise Lost*, 86.

Chapter 5

1. Zadie Smith, "Love Actually," *The Guardian*, October 31, 2003.
2. William Sharp, *Life and Letters of Joseph Severn* (London: Sampson, Low, Marston, 1892), 20–21.
3. Sharp, *Life and Letters*, 20.
4. William Hazlitt, *The Collected Works of William Hazlitt*, vol. 1, ed. A. R. Waller and Ronald Glover, intro. W. E. Henley (London: J. M. Dent, 1902), 77–79.
5. Hazlitt, *Collected Works*, 79.

Chapter 6

1. Haydon, *Life of Robert Benjamin Haydon*, 1:388.
2. I have followed Bates closely in this discussion of Hazlitt, *John Keats*, 256–59.
3. William Hazlitt, *Lectures on the English Poets* (London: Taylor and Hessey, 1818), 92.
4. See Friedrich Schlegel, *Philosophical Fragments*, trans. Peter Firchow (Minneapolis: University of Minnesota Press, 1991), 36, 45.

Chapter 7

1. Fitzgerald, *The Crack-Up*, 67.

Chapter 11

1. John Gibson Lockhart, "Cockney School of Poetry, No. IV," *Blackwood's Magazine* 3 (August 1818): 519–24
2. John Wilson Croker, "Review of Keats's *Endymion*," *Quarterly Review* 19 (April 1818): 204–8.
3. *John Keats: The Critical Heritage*, ed. G. M. Matthews (New York: Routledge, 1971), 94.

Chapter 12

1. I borrow this term from Victoria Nelson's *The Secret Life of Puppets* (Cambridge, Mass.: Harvard University Press, 2003), 110.
2. William Blake, "A Vision of the Last Judgment," in *The Complete Poetry and Prose of William Blake*, rev ed., ed. David Erdman, comm. Harold Bloom (New York: Anchor, 1982), 566.
3. Blake, "A Vision," 566.

Chapter 13

1. Thomas Medwin, *The Life of Percy Bysshe Shelley*, 2 vols. (London: Thomas Cautly Newby, 1847), 2:90.

Chapter 16

1. In my discussion of Dewey, I follow closely Thomas M. Alexander's *John Dewey's Theory of Art, Experience, and Nature: The Horizons of Feeling* (Albany: State University of New York Press, 1987), especially 197–99, where Alexander invokes Keats in his chapter on Dewey's *Art as Experience*.

Chapter 23

1. William Blake, "The Grey Monk," in *The Complete Poetry and Prose of William Blake*. I am thankful to the anonymous reader for Northwestern University Press who suggested this Blake connection.

INDEX

Abbey, Richard, 3, 10, 15, 47
Abrams, M. H., 49
allegory, vii, 5, 6, 39, 99; allegorical living, 99–100; *Endymion* and, 30, 32
ambiguity, 3
Apuleius, 117
artistic creation, 6–7, 23, 26–27, 91–92, 119, 122, 127–28

Bailey, Benjamin, 15, 25, 27–29, 40, 48, 57, 62, 73, 99
Bates, W. Jackson, 34
"Belle dame sans mercy, La" (Alain Chartier), 104, 105
Berryman, John, 34, 114
Blake, William, 32, 84, 92, 131, 149
Boccaccio, 57
Brawne, Fanny, 3, 17–18, 95–98, 100, 102, 103, 141, 152–53
Brown, Charles, vii, 15, 59–62, 68–70, 95–96, 110, 142, 151, 153
Browning, Tod, 91
Burns, Robert, 61
Byron, George Gordon, Lord, 34, 44–45, 100

Camus, Albert, 102
Caravaggio, Michelangelo Merisi da, 93, 147
Celtic mythology, 12
Chapman, George, 11, 13
Chatterton, Thomas, 101–2
Clarke, Charles Cowden, 9, 10, 11, 13–14
Claude Lorrain, 36
Coleridge, Samuel Taylor, 16–17, 19, 45, 80, 82, 90, 100, 141
Cooper, Astley, 10
Cox, Jane, 74–75, 76, 96, 97

Dante Alighieri, 17, 32, 68, 106
Dead Ringers, 63
depression, 10, 16–17, 18, 20, 33, 34, 39, 57, 67, 81, 102, 114–15, 131, 138–39, 148

Dewey, John, 113
Dickinson, Emily, 32, 54, 71, 73, 114
Dilke, Charles, 3–4, 37, 95–96
disinterestedness, 40–46

Elgin Marbles, 16, 19, 22
Eliot, T. S., 4
Emerson, Ralph Waldo, 93, 114
empathy, 3, 25–26, 34, 35, 37, 40–41, 51, 63, 80, 81, 93, 102, 115, 124, 148, 149, 154; reading and, 113
escapism, 12, 13, 34, 107, 110 ,131–32, 135, 137–38
Everyman, 6, 99

failure, 22, 44
fancy, 100–101, 118, 138–39
Faraday, Michael, 34
Fingal's Cave, 68–69, 92, 97
Fitzgerald, F. Scott, 5, 11, 54, 141
flexibility, 3, 32, 37
Forster, E. M., 31
Freud, Lucian, 91

genius: Keats on, 26, 37
Goethe, Johann Wolfgang von, 99
grace, 59, 68, 71, 110, 131, 142, 146

Hamilton, Sandi, 16, 17, 147, 149
Haydon, Robert Benjamin, 14, 15, 25, 39–40, 42, 52, 115
Hazlitt, William, 15, 36, 39, 40–41, 50, 59, 60
Hessey, James Augustus, 77–78, 153
Homer, 11–13
humor vs. wit, 36–37
Hunt, Leigh, 13–14, 16, 25, 39–40, 41, 42, 45, 77, 115

imagination, 4, 11, 18, 26–27, 34, 40, 43, 51–54, 59, 71, 76–77, 110, 136–38, 153–54
indolence, 42–44, 121
intensity, 35–37
irony, 44–45, 46, 52

James, William, 6, 7
Jones, Isabella, 74, 75–76, 96

Keats, George (and Georgiana), 9, 10, 16,
    47, 57, 63, 74–76, 77, 96, 99, 101, 106,
    110, 117, 151
Keats, John: critical reception, 14, 16,
    18, 77–78, 153; death of, 15, 17, 63,
    102, 147–48, 152–54; early life, 9–11;
    height, 74; illnesses, 3, 57, 61–63,
    71, 74, 77, 102, 151; journalism, 3;
    medical training, 9, 10–11, 15, 26, 53,
    58, 63; parents, 3, 9–10; personality,
    viii, 3, 10–11, 95; sense of humor,
    41–42, 50, 73–74; siblings, 3, 9–10,
    47–48, 77; suicidal tendencies, 3,
    10, 101–2, 103, 110, 137, 145, 151;
    women and, 73–76, 95, 100. WORKS:
    "Belle Dame sans Merci, La," 110–11;
    "Bright Star," vii, 60, 149; *Endymion*,
    16, 25, 29–32, 35, 39, 41, 46, 77–78,
    81, 101; *Eve of St. Agnes, The*, 95,
    103–7, 110, 137; *Fall of Hyperion, The*,
    107; "Great Spirits Are Now on Earth
    Sojourning," 14, 15; *Hyperion*, 17,
    83–92, 95, 97, 103–4, 110; *Isabella*, 39,
    57–58; "I Stood Tip-toe," 16; *Lamia*,
    142; *Lamia, Isabella, The Eve of St.
    Agnes, and Other Poems*, 153; "Ode on
    a Grecian Urn," 51, 117, 125–29, 131,
    135; "Ode on Indolence," 117, 121–24,
    131, 140; "Ode on Melancholy," 117,
    131–33, 135; "Ode to a Nightingale,"
    17, 27, 55, 117, 135–40, 141; "Ode
    to Psyche," 30, 117–19, 122, 123–24,
    131, 133; "On a Dream," 106, 110;
    "On First Looking into Chapman's
    Homer," 11–13, 14, 19, 20, 52, 80–81;
    "On Seeing the Elgin Marbles," 19–22,
    52, 71, 101; "On Sitting Down to Read
    King Lear Again," 41; "O Solitude!,"
    13; "On Visiting the Tomb of Burns,"
    61; *Otho the Great*, 142; *Poems*, 16,
    18; "Sleep and Poetry," 16; "Staffa,"
    69; "To Autumn," 3, 117, 141–46, 151;
    "When I Have Fears That I May Cease
    to Be," 45–46, 101, 149; "Why Did
    I Laugh Tonight," 95, 100–101, 106,
    110, 149
Keats, Thomas, 9, 39, 47–48, 57, 61, 74,
    77, 83, 84, 95–96; letters to, 59–60, 62,
    68–70, 97
Keats House, vii, 17–18, 93

Keats-Shelley House, 147–48
knowledge, 31. 32, 40, 43–44, 52–54,
    81–82, 89, 101, 114

Lake District, vii, 59–60, 63–64
Lamb, Charles, 39
Levi, Primo, 114
Lewis, C. S., 18–19
Lovecraft, H. P., 69
Lucas, William, 10

Martin, Steve, 42
melancholy, 18–19, 30, 89–90, 114,
    131–33
Melville, Herman, 5, 22, 33–34, 144
memento mori theme, 46, 64, 67–68, 101,
    133
Milton, John, 17–18, 23, 48, 69, 83–86,
    115
mist metaphor, 48, 50, 54, 60–61, 143,
    154
moments (and transience), 4, 7, 13, 27, 34,
    44, 59–60, 87–88, 90, 92, 100, 116;
    "moments of being," 60
Morris, William, 19
Murray, Bill, 32

Napoleon Bonaparte, 74
negative capability, 4–5, 31–37, 42–43, 46,
    48, 51, 67, 81, 113, 121, 139–40
Nietzsche, Friedrich, 6, 7, 36

Ollier, Charles, 16

Plato, 5–6
poetry, Keats on, 45, 48, 78–79, 121–22;
    on poetic fame, 46, 101
Prudentius, 6
psychotopography, 84

Reynolds, John Hamilton, 15, 24, 40–41,
    42, 44, 50, 53, 62, 74–75, 97, 110, 142
Reynolds, Marian, 99
Ritchie, Joseph, 39

Schlegel, August William and Friedrich
    von, 44
Severn, Joseph, 15, 35, 147–48, 153–54
Sexton, Anne, 114
Shakespeare, William, 10, 15, 22, 25, 29,
    33–37, 40, 46, 48, 100, 114, 115, 141,
    145; *As You Like It*, 100; *Cymbeline*,
    79; *Hamlet*, 5, 7, 9, 23, 52, 55, 84;

King Lear, 25, 33–34, 36, 41, 45, 154;
  Macbeth, 4, 45; *A Midsummer's Night
  Dream*, 41, 43; *Othello*, 79, 100; *The
  Tempest*, 100
Shelley, Percy Bysshe, 14, 41, 78, 84
Smith, Zadie, 31
solipsism, 25, 50–52, 55
soul, 5–6, 139; "soul-making," 109–10,
  111–15, 145, 152
Spenser, Edmund, 4, 6, 10, 99
Stevens, Wallace, 6, 7
strange, Keats on the, 97–98, 121
suicide. *See under* Keats, John
symbolism, defined, 99

Tarkovsky, Andrei, 91
Taylor, John, 45, 110, 153
Tennyson, Alfred, Lord, 12, 139
Thomas à Kempis, 115
Titian, 36, 37

truth (and beauty), 26–27, 36, 82, 127–28,
  141

Van Gogh, Vincent, 91

Welles, Orson, 93
West, Benjamin, 35–36, 37
Whitman, Walt, vii, 32, 43
Wilson, Una, vii, 16, 17–18, 19, 33–34, 64,
  92–93, 115, 141, 147–49
Woodhouse, Richard, 78–79, 84, 110
Woolf, Virginia, 5, 60, 114
Wordsworth, William, 14, 15, 32, 39,
  59, 63, 65, 84, 86; on "burden of the
  Mystery," 53–54; egotism, 42, 45, 79;
  height, 74; on "wise passivity," 140

Yeats, William Butler, 141

Zen, 93, 128